...es of the Unexpected

Wales

of the Unexpected

Richard Holland

ISBN: 1-84527-008-8

Cover illustration: Willy Pogany
Cover design: Sian Parri

First published in 2005 by
Gwasg Carreg Gwalch, 12 Iard yr Orsaf, Llanrwst,
Wales LL26 0EH.
℡ 01492 642031   ▤ 01492 641502
✆ books@carreg-gwalch.co.uk
Website: www.carreg-gwalch.co.uk

To Alan –
for dealing with the unexpected

Acknowledgements

I would like to thank *the North Wales Daily Post* for running the 'Wales of the Unexpected' column in its pages and for granting permission to publish this book based upon its contents. Special thanks go to Jill Tunstall for all her help over the years, and especially for being the one to come up with the clever title of *Wales of the Unexpected*. Thanks are also offered to the many readers who took the trouble to write in and tell me of their extraordinary experiences – indicating just what an unexpected place Wales is.

Biography

For eighteen years Richard Holland has been researching and writing about Welsh folklore and collecting stories of supernatural encounters in Wales. As well as the 'Wales of the Unexpected' column in the *North Wales Daily Post*, Richard has written a weekly column, 'Curiosities', in the Flintshire and Chester *Chronicle* and another called 'History and Mystery' in the *Denbighshire Free Press*, the *Rhyl Journal*, the County Pioneer and others. His previous books have included three with Gwasg Carreg Gwalch: *Supernatural Clwyd; the Folk Tales of North-East Wales, Haunted Wales, Bye-gones*, as well as *Haunted Wales*: *A Survey of Welsh Ghostlore*, with Landmark Publishing. He has also lectured widely on the subject of Welsh folklore.

Sources of the Stories

Many of the books I have used as reference material are out of print but most have been reprinted in the past and can be found second-hand reasonably cheaply. Here is a brief list of older works on Welsh folklore in chronological order.

The Cambrian Popular Antiquities by Peter Roberts (London, 1815)

Cambrian Superstitions by William Howells (Tipton, 1831)

British Goblins by Wirt Sikes (Sampson Low, 1880)

Welsh Folklore by Elias Owen (Wrexham and Oswestry, 1896)

Celtic Folklore by John Rhys (Clarendon Press, 1901)

Folk-Lore and Folk-Stories of Wales by Marie Trevelyan (Elliott Stock, 1909)

Folk-lore of West and Mid-Wales by J. Ceredig Davies (Aberystwyth, 1911)

Welsh Folklore and Folk Custom by T Gwynn Jones (Methuen, 1930)

All the above books are in English, although most are by Welsh-speaking authors. Welsh language books on the subject often contain a great deal of material translated from these English language sources. One notable exception is *Cymru Fu*, an anonymously gathered collection of romanticised folk tales published by Hughes and Son, Wrexham, in 1862. *Coelion Cymru* by Evan Isaac (Y Clwb Llyfrau Cymreig, 1938) also contains some interesting original material.

More fruitful are the Welsh language periodicals,

particularly *Y Brython* and the various National Eisteddfod 'transactions'. The English language periodical B*ye-gones* is especially rich in unique material on Welsh folk beliefs, and the publications of regional historical societies are also well worth examining.

Two other works I have consulted for *Wales of the Unexpected* are *Beddgelert: Its Facts, Fairies and Folklore* by D.E. Jenkins (Llewelyn Jenkins, 1899), and *The Book of South Wales* by Mr and Mrs Hall (Virtue and Co., 1861), but there are many, many more.

The subject of ghosts has been rather neglected in Wales, especially when compared to England and Scotland. I have sought to redress this with my publication of *Haunted Wales* (Landmark Publishing, 2005). A mix of old and new stories appears in *Ghosts of Wales* by Peter Underwood (Christopher Davies, 1978; Corgi, 1980) and Russell Gascoigne's *The Haunting of Glamorgan and Gwent* (Gwasg Carreg Gwalch, 1993) is an excellent resource.

Contents

A Glossary of Welsh Place-names 12

Introduction 13

Ghosts

    Great place for ghosts 16

    Dogging your footsteps 18

    The maiden's cry 21

    Haunted hostelries 23

    The mysterious imps 25

    Departed pets 27

    Unclean creatures 29

    The ghost-layers 31

    Stone's throw 34

    Ghost night 36

Omens of death

    Doomed to die 40

    Dark lights 43

    The death cry 46

    Community spirits 48

Fairies

    Do you believe in fairies? 68

    At home with the fairies? 70

    Around Bron Bannog 72

    Village fays 75

    Surf and turf 78

    Home help 80

    Fairies from space 82

Changelings 84

The Green Meadows of Enchantment 86

A mermaid 88

Monsters

Here be dragons 92

The lurker in the lake 96

Serpent ahoy! 99

Crocodile cave 102

Blood suckers 104

Witchcraft and magic

The oldest fear 108

Rough justice 110

Curses! 113

Charmed, I'm not so sure 115

The Pig o' the Brook 117

Weather retort 119

Making an impression 122

Mysterious monuments

Mysterious Island 126

Stones of power 129

Two neglected monuments 132

The Welsh pyramids 135

A mountain of legend 138

Great evil overcome 141

The home of Arthur 143

Old customs and other survivals

Sacred waters 148

Christmas customs 152

An end and a beginning 154
The cuckoo's call 156
Bride or bribe? 158
Pagan to Christian 160

Strange phenomena

Close encounters 166
Dreams come true 170
In the dark 172
Old flames 175

Stories from my readers

Readers write in 178
The ghost at the crossroads 181
Two black dogs and a haunted wood 183
Weird Wrexham 185
Small spirits 187
The man in 'fancy dress' 189
The man in the brown coat 190
The High Street puritan 191
Grave concerns 193
The lady in the lake 195
More from Tal-y-sarn 197
By the way, your house is haunted 199
Nightmare of a dream home 201
The girl in the blue gown 203
The wicked John Bodvol 205
In two places at once 207
The Ceffyl Dŵr 210
The Horror of Llofft Pinc 212

A glossary of Welsh place-names

Anglesey	*Ynys Môn*
Barmouth	*Bermo*
Beaumaris	*Biwmares*
Brecon	*Aberhonddu*
Colwyn Bay	*Bae Colwyn*
Dee	*Dyfrdwy*
Deeside	*Glannau Dyfrdwy*
Denbigh	*Dinbych*
Devil's Bridge	*Pontarfynach*
Holywell	*Treffynnon*
Menai Bridge	*Porthaethwy*
Menai Strait	*Afon Menai*
Mold	*Yr Wyddgrug*
Neath	*Castell-nedd*
Red Wharf Bay	*Traeth Coch*
Ruthin	*Rhuthun*
Snowdon	*Yr Wyddfa*
Solva	*Solfach*
St Asaph	*Llanelwy*
St David's	*Tyddewi*
Swansea	*Abertawe*
Tenby	*Dinbych-y-pysgod*
Vale of Glamorgan	*Bro Morgannwg*
Welshpool	*Y Trallwng*
Whitford	*Chwitffordd*
Wrexham	*Wrecsam*

Introduction

Wales is a most unexpected place. The strange, shadowy figures that inhabit its folklore – ghosts, goblins, fairies – are not yet dead – at least, not in the imaginations of its people. Wales has retained its mystery and its magic.

In this book I retell tales from the breadth of Wales's rich folklore. In these pages you will meet fairies, mermaids, witches, conjurers, phantom funerals, corpse candles and all manner of other apparitions, as well as many lively human characters and strange events from the fringes of Welsh history.

Not all these stories are old beliefs in the supernatural is still strong in Wales. Many readers of my weekly column in the North Wales Daily Post, on which this book is based, were able to furnish me with accounts of apparitions and other weird phenomena which had been witnessed within living memory – or which they had witnessed themselves. What they reported having seen often harks back to legend. These include accounts of a phantom white horse, spectral dogs, a malevolent green goblin, a restless spirit wandering to a graveyard in which its body should have been buried, and a strange little structure found in the heart of a lonely forest which was described as a 'fairy house'.

Wales of the Unexpected consists of retellings of legends, folk belief, and modern accounts of encounters with the unexpected. These are divided into sections dealing with such subjects as mysterious places, legendary creatures, fairy beliefs, witchcraft and ghostlore. Finally, there is a section devoted to fascinating stories supplied by my readers. The book ends with a particularly unnerving story which I publish here for the first time.

Wales of the Unexpected demonstrates one thing about Wales – it is always as well to expect the unexpected.

Ghosts

Great place for ghosts

A haunted castle is one of the staples of gothic romance. Ewloe, at Wepre Park on Deeside, really fits the bill – not only is it reputedly haunted by more than one ghost, but it is also buried deep in a gloomy wood.

The history of Ewloe castle is a bit murky. It is thought that the best preserved part of the building, the imposing Welsh Tower, is the oldest portion, built in the early thirteenth century by Llywelyn Fawr *(the Great)*, and that the castle was completed in about 1257 by Llywelyn ap Gruffudd after he recaptured the area from the English.

Ewloe's siting on low-lying ground in the heart of a wood puts it in a very weak defensive position. Such a position is almost unique, making the castle a real curiosity. Its odd location seems to have been chosen for secrecy. As historians have pointed out: 'The castle is not seen until the visitor is close upon it, and it was doubtless the purpose of its builders to conceal its presence as much as possible.'

The ghost of Ewloe castle is described as a glowing female figure who climbs the Welsh Tower during thunderstorms and there sings in a high, unearthly voice. Strange lights have also been seen around the ruin.

Teenager Chris Preece, of Buckley, told me that one night he and his uncle heard the unmistakable sounds of drumming and the stamping of feet marching to the castle, although there was no one to be seen. Was this an echo of the final battle at Ewloe, when the English army routed the forces of the unfortunate Llywelyn ap Gruffudd?

One of the most dramatic ghost stories from northern Wales

centres on Rhuddlan castle. The impressive walls (alas the castle is nothing more than a shell behind them) harbour a legend of devilish doings first written down (as far as I can tell) in 1803.

The yarn tells of a Princess Erilda and her infatuation with a mysterious man, the Warrior Knight of the Blood Red Plume, who is named after his stylish head-gear. Erilda is set to marry the Prince of Deheubarth, a marriage that would unite Wales in one strong alliance. But alas: Erilda falls under the spell of the Warrior Knight and agrees to elope with him.

All too soon she realises her mistake – her lover is in fact 'an agent of the infernal' (as he calls himself). He is a demon. As well as betraying Erilda, the Warrior Knight also contrives the death of her father, and the whole sorry affair serves to keep Wales in a state of discord, as was his purpose. Laughing cruelly, the Warrior Knight reveals his true form: that of a hideous scaly monster. He stabs poor Erilda through the heart with a trident and then sinks below the waters of the river Clwyd.

The legend ends by stating that Rhuddlan castle remains haunted by the spirit of the foolish Erilda, pursued for all eternity by the demonic Warrior Knight of the Blood Red Plume.

Sources: *Chester Ghosts and Poltergeists* by Charles Fairclough; Chris Preece, personal communication with the author; and *Welsh Legends*, anon., 1803. See plates 1 and 2.

Dogging your footsteps

One of the strangest yet most widespread apparitions reported in old books is that of the Black Dog, a huge hound-like beast said to haunt lonely lanes and crossroads at night.

The Black Dog has been recorded from all parts of the UK and elsewhere in the world. Usually the dogs resemble hounds of the mastiff variety and are often described as being as big as a calf. As their name suggests, they are usually black in colour and often they have great, glaring eyes.

In Wales the name Gwyllgi has been attached to them, a word meaning something like 'twilight dog'. The folklorist T. Gwynn Jones, writing in 1930, reported that his own grandmother had seen one of these horrors in Denbighshire:

'My grandmother declared that as she and my grandfather were riding on horseback from Ruthin one evening, in passing a roadside house, the nag suddenly shied and pressed to the hedge. At that moment a very tall mastiff was passing on the other side. My grandfather, who rode behind, saw nothing and his horse had not been startled. They had just come to live in the district and only got to know afterwards that the house had the reputation of being haunted.'

Unfortunately Jones does not say where precisely this haunted house stood.

A more startling account of such an encounter was reported in the 1920s by a former sergeant in the Denbighshire Yeomanry, one Edward Jones, who lived in the wild, southern part of the county.

Jones was returning on horseback from the fair at Cynwyd. As he crossed over the moors to his lonely farm, he suddenly realised he was being followed by a Gwyllgi, 'a beast of fearsome visage and blood-shot eye', as he described it. The creature – which he referred to by the dramatic name of the 'Black Hound of Destiny' – literally dogged his footsteps, or rather those of his horse. It was following 'just astern . . . ready for the spring, but never quite achieving the awaited climax as in the horrible, cold sweat anguish of a nightmare'. At last, a relieved Jones reached his home unmolested by the monster.

Reports of similar Black Dogs haunting Dartmoor in Devon inspired Arthur Conan Doyle's celebrated Sherlock Holmes novel *The Hound of the Baskervilles*. It is intriguing that Dartmoor is now said to be 'haunted' by big black cats, glimpsed at night, their eyes shining in the darkness. Perhaps these black cats are no more natural than the Black Dogs; perhaps they, too, are apparitions . . . for none have ever been caught.

Arguably the strangest Gwyllgi on record is that encountered in an overgrown lane in the Vale of Glamorgan. A farm servant described his encounter with the spectre some time prior to the year 1839. At first, he said, he saw two large, bright, moonlike eyes, approaching. When it came closer he saw that the apparition's head and shoulders seemed to be those of a man but its body and limbs were like those of a large spotted dog. He struck out at it with the only thing to hand – his hat – but he felt nothing.

Sources: *Welsh Folklore and Folk Custom* by T. Gwynn Jones; the 1929 volume of *Bye-gones; The Vale of Glamorgan* by John Redwood. See also Richard Holland, *Haunted Wales*, published by Landmark, for much more on Black Dogs.

The maiden's cry

An enduring old legend from northern Wales is that of a body of water haunted by the pitiful wailing of its resident ghost.

The name of this famous haunted spot is Llyn Nad-y-Forwyn *(the lake of the maiden's cries)*. This name cannot be found on the map today and it has taken me some time to locate it. When the folklorist Elias Owen wrote about it in 1896 he too was unaware of its location and assumed it was a full-sized lake. However, I recently discovered the 'llyn' is not a lake at all, but a deep pool in Afon Colwyn (*afon*: river), just north of Beddgelert. Here is Owen's version of the legend:

'It is said that a young man was about to marry a young girl, and on the evening before the wedding they were rambling along the water's side together, but the man was false and loved another better than the woman he was about to wed. They were alone in an unfrequented country, and the deceiver pushed the girl into the lake to get rid of her to marry his sweetheart.

'She lost her life. But ever afterwards her spirit troubled the neighbourhood, but chiefly the scene of her murder. Sometimes she appeared as a ball of fire, rolling along the Afon Colwyn, at other times she appeared as a lady dressed in silk, taking a solitary walk along the banks of the river.

'At other times groans and shrieks were heard coming out of the river – just such screams as would be uttered by a person who was being murdered. Sometimes a young maiden would be seen emerging out of the waters, half naked, with dishevelled hair that covered her shoulders, and the country resounded with her heart-rending crying as she appeared in the lake. The frequent crying of the Spirit gave to the lake its name, Llyn Nad-y-Forwyn.'

A book about Beddgelert published in 1899 nails the location – a place called Llam Trwsgwl *(stumbling leap)*. This is a place where the river narrows between two steep rocks, which forces the water through. Young men would sometimes use this perilous place to jump the river – hence the name. But this was dangerous because immediately beyond the 'stumbling leap' is a deep pool with slippery sides, which is difficult to climb out of.

It was into Llam Trwsgwl that the poor girl was pushed and it was this pool that she subsequently haunted. Just south of the pool is an environment agency hut and a small weir. The many danger notices here warning of strong currents and deep water show that Llyn Nad-y-Forwyn is still a dangerous place.

Today it is overhung with trees, shrubs and other vegetation, making it darker and spookier than it was a century ago, and unfortunately impossible to photograph. Strangely, on my ramble in search of the pool, it was a weird cry I heard coming from the undergrowth which led me to it. The cry may have been that of a bird, or perhaps a fox. Perhaps . . .

Sources: *Welsh Folklore* by Elias Owen; *Welsh Folklore and Folk Custom* by T. Gwynn Jones; *Beddgelert: Its Facts, Fairies and Folklore* by D.E. Jenkins. See Plate 33.

Haunted hostelries

Although ruined castles and creepy old mansions are considered the most likely places to be haunted, many humbler buildings are, too.

Among the most haunted houses are public houses. Perhaps we should not be surprised by this – pubs have seen a lot of life (and death) and many old inns have romantic tales attached to them. And it's possible restless spirits are attracted to places where they felt happy in life.

Many licensees have experienced eerie phenomena. Some years ago the landlord of the Pwllgwyn, a pub and restaurant near Caerwys, in Flintshire, reported that his staff sometimes saw a phantom monk sitting quietly by a window, often in daylight.

The Pwllgwyn is said to stand on the site of a medieval pilgrims' hostelry, which might explain his presence. Mind you, his behaviour could be far from monkish – on one occasion the landlord felt an invisible handle fondle his bottom!

But this ghostly assault is nothing compared to that suffered by a brewery area manager at the Golden Lion in Rossett, Wrexham. This level-headed man decided to sleep in a certain room to help dispel its growing reputation for being haunted. He ended up having a fight with an invisible entity – they had a tug-of-war over the frightened man's bedclothes. The entity won.

However, stories of haunted pubs should be taken with a pinch of salt, especially when a new landlord has taken over. Too often a pub suddenly becomes 'haunted', and is promoted as such in the papers, with a picture of the landlord grinning under a headline which usually trots out a joke about 'spirits after hours'.

Friends of mine ran a Flintshire pub back in the 1980s and the place seemed to become haunted after some building work was carried out. Occasionally they glimpsed an ill-defined apparition, apparently of a man, which emerged from a blocked-up doorway before drifting through the bar. This was the only ghost they saw.

By the time my friends moved elsewhere, the pub was well-known as haunted (which was partly my fault, of course, for repeating it). It was interesting to note over the years that with each new landlord who took over the license, new ghosts appeared – female apparitions, a man smoking a pipe, and spectral children playing in the cellar.

Credible witnesses told me of seeing some of these apparitions, so they may not all have been inventions. Nevertheless, I couldn't help smiling when I was told of the latest ghost – a Roman soldier in the bar.

This latter was suggested by a 'medium' who was busy plying his trade in the lounge bar next door. When I expressed my doubts about this manifestation, I was later told the medium had meant 'a roaming soldier'.

Source: Personal communications with the author. For more on haunted pubs see *Haunted Clwyd*.

The mysterious imps

An interesting little story about an allegedly haunted house at Llanfyllin, Powys, appeared in an 1835 number of the charmingly titled magazine *The Cabinet For Youth*. The magazine explained that a man named Thomas, who is described as a 'supervisor of excise', needed to find a house to let in Llanfyllin, but the only one available was a big, dilapidated old place called Tŷ Gwyn. The rent was very low, however, which was some compensation, so Thomas took it.

He moved in on his own at first, perhaps because he wanted to spend some time on repairs before sending for his family, or perhaps because, since taking it, he had learnt why the house was in such poor condition and why the rent was so low – it was haunted.

Thomas spent the first night in Tŷ Gwyn quite peacefully, but on the second he was disturbed by some rather sinister sounds. He could hear pitter-pattering outside his door, 'running, as of imps, up and down the stairs'. Thomas was brave enough to go and investigate, but could find nothing to account for the noises.

The following evening he laid sand all over the stairs, in the hope that whatever he was sharing his house with would leave some traces. That night, from his bed, he could hear the same sinister pitter-pattering, and the light of morning revealed the traces that he had hoped for – or perhaps dreaded. In the sand on the stairs Thomas found the prints of numerous little cloven feet!

A practical sort of chap, Thomas was determined that no devils, never mind how many of them there might be, would frighten him away, and he even had the audacity to lay down some traps. That night he took the further precaution of arming himself with a brace of pistols. He waited in the dark and in time heard again the sounds of tiny feet running up and own the stairs. Then he heard several loud shrieks as the traps were sprung!

Pistols at the ready, Thomas tore over to the staircase and there he found – three fat rabbits.

It turned out Tŷ Gwyn was being invaded by rabbits from a nearby warren. The bunnies' burrowing had brought them into communication with the building's sewerage system, and they had been making their way in ever since. Thomas was therefore relieved to find that not only had he acquired a house at a very advantageous rent but he also had the benefit of all the rabbits he could eat!

Source: The 1907 volume of *Bye-gones*.

Departed pets

A friend of mine, Wendy, used to live near Afon-wen, in Flintshire. She told me that when she was a little girl she had a pet hamster. Sadly, as all pets do one day, it died. The night after her hamster was laid to rest, Wendy woke up to hear a sound coming from the corner of her bedroom. It was a sound she knew well – it was the rattling of her deceased pet's wheel turning round in its cage.

Bemused, the sleepy child raised her head from her pillow and looked into the corner of her room. Inside the hamster cage she could see the wheel spinning round and round – and inside the wheel there was a small, hamster-sized ball of light!

It's a comforting thought that our beloved pets may have an afterlife to go to. There are many stories on record of human ghosts being accompanied by their pets. Madam Godolphin, an arrogant, not very likeable lady of the eighteenth century, was said to haunt the area around Llansantffraid in Powys. Sometimes her ghost would be seen sitting on a stile, always with the ghost of her little dog sitting beside her. Perhaps this faithful animal was her only friend in the Beyond.

Nearer the present day there is the story of a former colleague, Geoff Ellis, who told me about the ghost of a dog which haunted his cottage in Mynydd Isa, near Mold. It was an indistinct shape and usually accompanied by the equally vague figure of a person, possibly a little old lady:

'Occasionally, I get a glimpse of it walking through the living room [but] usually I just hear it pattering upstairs,' he said.

I was told the strangest story of a ghost pet a long time ago, before I started keeping records of these stories, and so my memory of it is sketchy. I know the chap who told me his experience was called Nigel and I am fairly certain that the cottage he was renting was in Deeside. Despite the uncertainty of details, it's worth recording here since it hasn't been recorded elsewhere.

Nigel started renting an old cottage and soon found he had many friendly neighbours – the local cats, which would daily gather at his back door. He guessed the former occupant used to feed them, so he put down a saucer of milk on the step and watched his new friends lap it up. But one day, he put the saucer down just inside the door – and the cats wouldn't touch it. They stared longingly at their treat but seemed too scared to come in. He soon found out why.

The house was already occupied by a cat – a ghost one! A few weeks after moving in, Nigel saw it regularly and in all parts of the cottage. He'd catch glimpses of it in his bedroom and in his living room, a sleek shape vanishing out of the corner of his eye. Then one evening, while he was quietly watching television, the phantom moggie walked across the room – and straight through his outstretched legs!

Sources: Personal communication with author; the 1877 volume of *Bye-gones*; see also *Haunted Clwyd*.

Unclean creatures

People using a lane near Pentrefoelas, in Conwy, would sometimes find themselves being followed by the apparition of a black pig which would come trotting out of a ruin. Anyone who objected to being pursued by a phantom porker might strike out at it with their stick, but the stick would pass right through it and on it would come just the same.

For a long time pigs were associated with the devil. When Edmund Jones – an early writer on the supernatural in Wales – was told a friend in Monmouthshire had been bothered by an evil spirit that squeaked like a pig, he commented that he wasn't surprised, since pigs were 'such unclean creatures'.

In the eighteenth century the grand house called Hafod – now demolished – near Devil's Bridge, in Ceredigion, was possessed by a particularly troublesome poltergeist. In 1759 the previously invisible spook took on physical form. First it appeared as 'a beautiful woman wanting to be kissed' and later as a pig. It was said that it affectionately 'rubbed against the master and mistress' of the house – but only in its swinish shape, which might have been a disappointment to the master of Hafod.

When an exorcism took place at Llanfor, Gwynedd, the spirit to be exorcised also took the form of a pig. It had invaded the church, so the exorcist rode his horse into the sacred building and brought the 'pig' out on the back of it. An old woman who witnessed this cried out: 'Duw annwyl! Mochyn yn yr eglwys' *(Good God! A pig in the church)*.

'On hearing these words,' writes Elias Owen, 'the pig

became exceedingly fierce, because the silence had been broken, and because God's name had been used, and in his anger he snatched up both the man and the mare, and threw them right over the church to the other side.'

The ghost was eventually 'laid' despite this hiccup, however.

Finally, a most impressive spectral swine is that which manifested itself long ago when the church of Llanfair Dyffryn Clwyd, Denbighshire, was being built. Every night an enormous pig's head would loom out of the darkness and demolish all the building work that had been carried out on the church during the day.

Eventually the builders took the hint and built the church in the place where it now stands. The original site is still locatable from the name of a nearby farm – Llanbenwch *(church of the pig's head)*.

Source: *Welsh Folklore and Folk Custom* by T. Gwynn Jones; *Welsh Folklore* by Elias Owen; *Old Stone Crosses in the Vale of Clwyd* by Elias Owen.

The ghost-layers

In 1777, the following advertisement appeared in a London newspaper:

'HAUNTED HOUSES. Whereas there are mansions and castles in England and Wales which have for many years been uninhabited, and are now falling to decay, by their being haunted and visited by evil spirits, or the spirits of those who for unknown reasons are rendered miserable even in the grave, a gentleman, who has made the tour of Europe, of a particular turn of mind and deeply skilled in the abstruse and sacred science of exorcism, hereby offers his assistance to any owner or proprietor of such premises, and undertakes to render the same free from the visitation of such spirits, be their cause what it may, and render them tenantable and useful to the proprietors. Letters addressed to the Rev. John Jones, No. 30 St Martin's-Lane, duly answered and interview if required. NB – Rooms rendered habitable in six days.'

Judging by the name, this man 'of a particular turn of mind' was a Welshman, and no wonder, for Wales is full of tales of 'ghost-layers', men employed to rid houses of evil spirits. They were like pest exterminators, but the pests were poltergeists rather than cockroaches.

Few, however, were bold enough to claim an exorcism after just six days. Often the spirits they were attempting to expel took terrifying forms – huge scary dogs, bulls, even lions.

In each case, the first thing the exorcist did to protect himself from their assaults was to draw a circle on the ground. Sometimes the circle was elaborated upon with magical symbols or enhanced by magical substances such as salt, but the important thing seemed to be the circle itself – if the exorcist stood inside it, the spirit would be kept on the outside.

There would then proceed a battle of wills. The exorcist would use prayers and spells to quell the ghost, to weaken its power. The ghost-layer would know he was winning when the apparition began to lose its fearsome appearance and shrink in size. If the ghost had first appeared as a big dog, for example, it would start to appear as smaller animals, until finally it might appear as a fly or a spider.

Bottles, goose-quills, tobacco boxes, even the Bible itself, might be employed to trap troublesome spooks. These were then buried, often under bridges, and a 'ban' would be placed upon the ghost. In the case of exorcisms at Llanidloes, in Powys, and Llandegla, in Denbighshire, the spirit would remain under their respective bridges until a sapling had gown tall enough to reach the parapet. In another case, a spirit had to chip away a huge outcrop of rock with a tin-tack. Another, banished to the Red Sea (a Biblical notion), was allowed to advance back to Wales at the rate of the length of one grain of wheat a year.

A collector of tales, D. E. Jenkins, interviewed a supposed ghost-layer in Beddgelert in the late nineteenth century. This man's allegedly first-hand description of an exorcism at a farm called Erw includes some interesting details.

'I made the mystical circle on the floor with salt,' he said, 'and drew the image of the cross in its centre. Then I entered the circle myself and stood between the arms of the cross in the customary way, reading the usual charm passage . . .' He did not elucidate on the 'charm' but he informed Jenkins that ghosts have 'grades'. The Erw ghost was of a very high grade – much higher than the exorcist first thought – and manifested itself as 'some hideous creature, not unlike a huge tiger'.

Ghost-layer and ghost stared each other out for a long time, the former demanding the latter to withdraw in the name of the cross. At length the dreadful spirit did withdraw and the exorcist immediately read out the correct charm for its grade. This had the desired effect and the ghost 'came back, licking the floor like a dog before his master'. The exorcist was then able to deal with it.

'If I had betrayed the least bit of fear, or if I had taken my eye off for the quarter of a second,' said the exorcist, 'I would have been done for.'

Sources: *Welsh Folklore* by Elias Owen and *Beddgelert, Its Facts, Fairies and Folklore* by D.E. Jenkins. For more Welsh exorcisms see *Haunted Wales*.

Stone's throw

Imagine your home has suddenly become a target for vandals: somebody keeps throwing stones at it, breaking windows and risking injury to your family. Now imagine you discover no *human* vandal is to blame, that the assailant turns out to be a malicious, invisible entity . . .

Such frightening incidents have been recorded all over the world and there have been several cases in Wales. Folklorist Elias Owen, for example, noted a haunting at a road near Caellwyngrydd, Bethesda. In 1896 he wrote: 'This was a dangerous spirit. People passing along the road were stoned by it; its work was always mischievous and hurtful.'

A farm near Pontrhydfendigaid, in Ceredigion, was said to be similarly haunted. In 1911 it was reported that a spirit there had 'engaged in the dangerous game of stone-throwing to the great discomfort of the family'.

A house called Bryn-glas at Llanfair Caereinion in Powys was another such site. A gentleman, writing in 1903, recorded: 'My father, in the early part of his career, took up residence at Bryn-glas. This was evidently at a period when the manifestations of the supposed ghost were at their height, for by day as well as by night, the mansion was being subjected to intermittent storms of missiles, but whence they came or by whom sped, remained undiscovered, and apparently undiscoverable.'

This 'dangerous game' seems linked to reports of poltergeist activity and often accompanies it. A famous poltergeist case centred on Hafod, a manor house now demolished, which used to stand near Devil's Bridge. One report recounts the following incident:

'A company of fifteen being in a room shut close, the hearth was filled with stones. A person put his foot on one stone to keep it secure. All the stones, including the one under the man's foot, were removed to the other end of the room.'

The most severe of the Welsh examples I have on record took place at Llanllechid, in Gwynedd. This village is a few miles from Bethesda, so the culprit may have been the same as that at Caellwyngrydd. The incident took place about the year 1758.

A farmhouse was regularly pelted with stones, but no visible person was ever seen throwing them. Most of the stones seemed to come from the river that flowed behind the house, for they were all worn smooth. Some of them were huge – one weighed twenty-seven pounds! The strangest detail in the case was that the missiles sometimes appeared *inside* the house and were thrown from one room to another.

Life became so unbearable that a party of clergymen from Bangor was called in to try and exorcise the presumed spirit, but they, too, were so severely pelted with rocks that they had to beat a hasty retreat. After this, the house was abandoned and no one lived there again.

Sources: *Welsh Folklore* by Elias Owen; *Folklore of West and Mid Wales* by J. Ceredig Davies; the 1903 volume of *Bye-gones; Apparitions of Spirits* by Edmund Jones.

Ghost night

All Hallows – All Saints' – Eve was the most important of the three 'ghost nights' in Welsh tradition (the others being the eve of May Day, and St John's Eve – June 23rd). On these nights it was believed that the boundaries between the physical and 'other' worlds became less defined.

Hallowe'en was the last night of the year in the old Celtic calendar and fires were lit in a tribute to the waning sun. In time, these fires were also seen as helping to ward off the spirits of the night. Today our bonfires are lit a few nights later, on November 5th, to commemorate the failure of the Gunpowder Plot. Interestingly, fireworks are also used to scare off ghosts in the Eastern cultures from which we imported them.

It was once considered dangerous to go out between midnight and dawn on Hallowe'en because spirits would be holding their carnival, free to do as they pleased. In the Vale of Clwyd they took the shape of little black pigs, according to Elias Owen, who quotes this rhyme in Welsh:

'Hwch ddu gwta,
Ar ben pob camdda,
Yn nyddu ac yn gardio
Pob Glan Gaua.'

Which translates as:

'A short-tailed black sow,
On every stile,
Spinning and carding,
Each All Hallows Eve'.

Pigs were considered 'unclean' animals, the eating of their flesh forbidden in the Old Testament Book of Leviticus (see also page 29). Stiles were popular hang-outs for spirits, because they are 'non-places' which lead to other places, like crossroads and bridges. The detail that the 'black sows' are seen spinning yarn takes us back to the ancient belief in the Fates, who would spin out the life of a man before snipping it with a pair of shears when he was due to die. All in all, a bizarre but eerie image.

With the spirit world so close on Hallowe'en night, it was the most popular night for 'rhamanta', or traditional Welsh divination. For example, young women would act out rituals intended to reveal to them their future husbands.

It was essential not to take these things lightly, however. One boy who interrupted some girls carrying out such divination had a horrible shock.

The girls had hung their undergarments on a line, in the belief that apparitions of young men would materialise and be seen to touch the garment belonging to the girl he would marry. A flesh-and-blood youth, however, had placed his shirt on the line as a joke and intended to rush out on the girls to frighten them.

But they were all very frightened when the spectre of a coffin appeared out of the darkness and was seen to float over to where the boy's shirt was hanging on the line. The boy emerged from his hiding place and tried to laugh off the apparition as a dream. Alas, he died not long after, when he fell off a bridge.

Sources: *Old Stone Crosses in the Vale of Clwyd* by Elias Owen; *Cambrian Superstitions* by William Howells.

Omens of death

Doomed to die

A weird encounter with the supernatural took place many years ago in the centre of Corwen, Denbighshire. Here is how the witness described it:

'I was coming home from a neighbouring village, when I heard wailing sounds a short distance in advance. I paused and listened, and suddenly found myself borne backward in a funeral procession. I distinctly saw the coffin and recognized one or two persons in the crowd beside me.

'With the procession I was borne on to the ancient parish church [of St Sulien and St Maen], and not far from the doorway saw a well-known Dissenting Minister approaching and joining us. Then the whole phantom vanished. I was greatly frightened, and on reaching home promptly related my experiences.

'About fourteen days later a friend of ours died in Corwen. I went to the funeral, and, arriving rather late, was pressed backward in the crowd. Near the old church a well-known Dissenting Minister joined the procession, and in it I recognized other people who appeared previously as phantoms.'

Strange though the man's experience was, it was far from unique. In Welsh folklore there is a great body of stories relating to omens of death. Phantom funerals which warn of real funerals to come are among the most widely reported of these supernatural warnings.

In the past, many Welsh people who found themselves having to tramp the lanes at night would be sure to keep close to the verge, rather than walk down the middle. This was because of their fear of encountering a phantom funeral. Not only was it considered an unnerving experience but also one that was potentially dangerous. It was better to keep out of their way. The following story from Tenby is a good example of the harm somebody could come to if they met a phantom funeral.

The manservant of the Rector of Penally was in love with a pretty servant girl at Holloway Farm, and he used to steal out at night to visit her. These meetings were heartily disapproved of by the Rector.

One November evening, coming home, this romantic fellow was passing the turn of the road which led from Holloway to Penally, when he saw a silent funeral procession approaching him. He pressed himself into the hedge to let the people pass by, but the mourners – some of whom he recognised – 'jostled so rudely against him, that they hurt and bruised him severely, not heeding his entreaties or cries'. At last, free of the brutal treatment he received from the phantoms, he watched the procession continue on a strange course: it went over a hedge into the next field, then made a detour, before returning over the same hedge further on.

The next morning he awoke bruised and sore and begged his master to give him a day off. The Rector refused to believe his servant's tale, however, and accused him of having been 'drinking and fighting' in an ale-house. Some weeks later, however, an incident occurred to prove the man's story was true.

Heavy snow had fallen and the weather was bitterly cold. The Holloway farmer died, and many followed his procession to Penally churchyard. The great snowdrifts confused the bearers, however, and they missed the road under its featureless white blanket, passing by mistake into the next field. They processed a little way through the field, the mourners following, until, realising their mistake, they came back onto the road, by the very same detour the manservant had witnessed three weeks previously.

Source: *Folk-Lore and Folk-Stories of Wales* by Marie Trevelyan; *The Book of South Wales* by Mr and Mrs Hall.

Dark lights

In the early years of the nineteenth century, a man named Evans lived in an old house by the walls of the churchyard in Silian, Ceredigion, and he was entrusted with the key to the church. One evening a young man came to the church to take part in a singing class. He was a little early but noticed there was a light on in the church, so he went to open the door, confident there was someone inside to receive him. However, he found the door locked and when he peeped in through the keyhole he saw that the building was in fact empty. Somewhat confused, he popped over to Mr Evans's house for the key, and mentioned to him that there was a light in the church.

'You must be making a mistake,' replied Mr Evans. 'There cannot possibly be any light in the church; no one could have entered the building to light it, for the door is locked, and I have the key here in the house.'

The young man being insistent on the fact, Evans accompanied him back to the church – and together they saw the light coming out of the church and then floating across the churchyard. Hurriedly, they followed the mysterious light until it suddenly disappeared into the ground.

Now the young man realised that what they had seen was a corpse candle. The cannwyll corff, as it is called in Welsh, is a mysterious light which warns of a coming death. Usually it would be seen floating towards a burial ground, following the route a funeral procession was soon to take. Sometimes it would be seen in the room of a person doomed to die.

The young man used a stick to mark the spot where the light had vanished. True to form, when there came to be a burial again in Silian, the spot chosen for the grave turned out to coincide with that previously chosen by the corpse candle.

A place between Solva and St David's, in Pembrokeshire, once became notorious for the appearance of these corpse candles – so much so that people began to avoid using the road after dark. Two farmers who had to pass by the haunted spot one night were therefore not surprised – but no less terrified – at seeing a cannwyll corff appear ahead of them. The pair had been 'drinking freely'. One was sober enough to run away from the light, but the other was so drunk he had no choice but to remain where he was and put his trust in fate.

The tale was recounted in 1861, by a Mrs Hall: 'The "candle" was approaching the very spot on which he stood. As it drew near, he saw that it was placed on a large coffin, which in its turn was carried on the shoulders of two persons in grave-clothes, as if recently risen from the dead. For a moment the man was staggered. The next instant he was sober. "If," thought he to himself, "thou art a spirit, thou wilt not molest me – on my brother's account, who is a clergyman; if thou art a devil, thou hast no business with me at present, since I am thine all in good time; but if thou art a man – why, heaven help thee, that's all!" – and he firmly grasped the large staff he carried in his hand.

'By the time he had finished reasoning thus with himself, the apparition was at his side; expecting, no doubt, the instant flight of the farmer, it marched past him with great dignity, but had not advanced three paces before the first spirit fell to the ground stunned from a blow of the heavy staff – the second spirit seemed to fear a similar fate, for it at once dropped his end of the coffin, and ran faster than most mortals usually run.

'The farmer was well rewarded for his courage. In the spirit that lay half dead at his feet he recognised a notorious thief who had long infested the neighbourhood with impunity, and who had been more than suspected of stealing the sheep which now and then for months past had been missing from the farmer's own folds. And so it was. The coffin contained two dead sheep, marked with his initials by his own hand. The thief, aided by an accomplice, trusting to the well-known superstitious feelings of the people, had hit upon this ingenious expedient.'

Sources: *Folklore of West and Mid Wales* by J. Ceredig Davies; *A Book of South Wales* by Mr and Mrs Hall.

The death cry

Martin Blane was an Irishman, one of many of his countrymen and women who worked in the Welsh fields as a haymaker. He was elderly and becoming increasingly feeble, and his one hope was that he would earn enough to be able to return to his native land before he died.

Because of his age, the farmer whom Blane worked for allowed him to stay in his barn for a few weeks while he gathered strength for his trip – but he grew weaker rather than stronger.

One night the farmer, whose room faced the barn, was startled by a wailing sound, 'loud and unearthly'. He hurried to his window and saw, crouching by the door of the barn, 'a female form shrouded from head to foot in a cloak . . . sobbing piteously'.

Over and over again this strange figure let out a blood-chilling, mournful wail and she frequently extended fleshless arms and clapped her hands with a hard, 'bony' sound. This went on for some time, and the farmer was rooted to the spot with fear:

'Suddenly the dark form arose – it was very tall and awful – folded its cloak around it close – close as a bat its wings, crying still, but faintly.'

It faded away in the darkness, the eerie wailing continuing for a little while longer. Then all was still. Snapping out of his trance, the farmer hurried outside. He found Martin Blane was dead and all his other servants 'crouched in one heap at his door'.

This story was written down by a traveller, Mrs Hall, in 1861. Unfortunately, she does not give a location for the weird adventure. However, she leaves no doubt as to the identity of the apparition – it was a banshee. Banshees are female spirits which belong to old families in Ireland, and which appear in order to warn of the deaths of any of the family members.

Wales had its own version of the banshee: the Gwrach y Rhibyn, which broadly translates as 'Hag of the Mists'. The Gwrach y Rhibyn also appeared as an old woman – a hideous one – and would wail and moan in grief in the same way as a banshee. A vivid eyewitness account of this apparition, seen in Llandaf, Cardiff, in 1877, describes it as 'a horrible old woman with long red hair and a face like chalk, and great teeth like tusks . . . she went through the air with a long black gown trailing along the ground below her arms.'

The Gwrach gave out an unearthly screech and flapped bat-like wings against the window of a neighbouring house – where a man was found dead the next morning.

Her visitation was intended as a warning – but the ghastly sight and sound of her was more likely to send this poor man to his grave than otherwise.

Sources: *The Book of South Wales* by Mr and Mrs Hall; *British Goblins* by Wirt Sikes.

Community spirits

In the crook of a little lane which winds its way through a sparsely populated corner of Flint Mountain can be found a pretty little pool of water. It's a charming spot, but one that had a very sinister reputation a hundred and fifty years ago.

This is the Pwll-y-Wrach *(the witch's pool)*. It was said that mysterious beings lived beneath its surface, creatures rather more dangerous than the usual newts or beetles. They looked just like humans but had strange powers, including the ability to foretell the future.

In the winter of 1852 a man named John Roberts encountered one of these entities, a meeting which had tragic consequences. John had just stepped out his front door when he found a youth whom he did not recognise barring his way. He asked him his business, but on receiving no reply, he tried to brush past him.

The boy grabbed him – and in one terrifying instant, John was hurled through the air and thrown into the mud on the edge of Pwll-y-Wrach. The strange youth held his face down until it was nearly touching the water and, struggle though he might, John could not escape his iron grip.

Then the being whispered in his ear: 'When the cuckoo sings its first note at Flint Mountain, I shall come again to fetch you,' and with that, it vanished.

John Roberts died the following May. He had been carrying out some building repairs when a wall collapsed and crushed him. A young woman who had witnessed the accident said that that it had happened just after she had noticed a cuckoo come to rest in a tree nearby.

As John's crushed body was carried home, the cuckoo

1. Creepy Ewloe Castle is hidden in a wood and has several spooky tales told about it.

2. A gothic legend involving a doomed romance and an agent of the Devil is set at Rhuddlan Castle.

3. The charming village of Llanelian-yn-Rhos was once the centre of a kind of Welsh voodoo cult.

4. The standing stone of Pant-y-Maen cast a spell over a farmer who impudently tried to use it as a gate post.

5. The mysterious 'thigh stone' was cemented into the wall of the ruinous church at Llanidan – to prevent it walking around!

6. At the Lligwy cromlech a sailor was given a lucky charm by a witch he had saved from drowning.

7. Moel Fama in the snow – during the severe winter of 1773 a story went round that this hill on the Flintshire-Denbighshire border had erupted like a volcano!

8. Near the white post in the centre of this picture a hideous little goblin appeared, startling a man walking his dog down the lane in the 1960s.

9. At 45ft high, the mysterious Gop Cairn is one of the biggest pre-historic mounds in Europe. Its function is unknown.

10. Anglesey's Barclodiad yr Gawres is one of the most impressive burial mounds in Britain.

11. Towering above the Vale of Llangollen, the fortified hill of Dinas Brân has many legends attached to it.

12. A wicked tyrant, Benlli Gawr, had his court in the Iron Age hillfort of Moel Fenlli.

13. From the ramparts of the hillfort on Moel Arthur, the May morning sun can be seen to rise above the hillfort of Caerfallwch in Flintshire. Both sites have links with the Arthurian Tradition.

14. Weird beings haunted the Pwll-yr-Wrach, or 'Witch's Pool', on Flint Mountain, spirits which had the ability to prophesy a person's death.

15. The ancestral spirits of Llantysilio congregated in the little parish church to pronounce the doom of the local squire.

16. Llyn Dywarchen – the 'Lake of the Turves' – once possessed a floating island (not the one in the picture). It was also a popular haunt of the fairies.

17. The wizard Myrddin saw two dragons fighting below the ancient fortress of Dinas Emrys – a vision of a great struggle to come for the Welsh nation.

18. The author examines the mighty standing stone of Post Coch, where a savage flying serpent met a nasty but well-deserved end. Picture: Scott Lloyd

19. Corpse candles were seen on several occasions about the year 1910 in Mawddach estuary. In 1975 a strange aquatic beast came crawling out of the estuary near Barmouth.

20. The interior of the church of Llangar, restored by Cadw (note the 18th Century figure of Death on the left). The isolated site of Llangar was said to have been dictated by the appearance of a holy white stag.

21/22 Corwen church appears to have been built on a pre-Christian sacred site. A standing stone has actually been incorporated into one of the walls (left), while a medieval preaching cross (right) has been set into a round slab bearing prehistoric 'cup and ring' markings.

23. Is Llyn Tegid – Bala Lake – inhabited by its own version of Scotland's Loch Ness Monster?

24. The waters of St Winefride's Well at Holywell (Treffynnon) have been resorted to for hundreds of years.

25. It is hard to believe today but the well of St Tegla was once famous. Its waters were believed to cure epilepsy, provided a weird and elaborate ritual was carried out.

26. Tucked away down a little country lane in Denbighshire, the enclosed well of Ffynnon Sara has a serene, almost holy, atmosphere.

27. The author admires the extraordinary preservation of the ancient huts on Tre Ceiri – the 'Town of the Giants' – one misty day in March.
Picture: Scott Lloyd

28. The huge boulders of Henblas Dolmen enclose a tiny prehistoric grave. Henblas Dolmen is one of the largest yet least known of Anglesey's ancient monuments.

29. Some Welsh heroes and saints have literally left their mark on the landscape. This footprint in a boulder near Corwen is said to have been made by Owain Glyndŵr. Picture: Fortean Picture Library

30. The early medieval wheel cross of Maen Chwyfan may be in such good preservation because it was able to protect itself – with bolts of lightning.

31. Along this lane on Anglesey a little boy and his father saw the Gwyllgi – the Dog of Darkness of Welsh folklore.

32. Handsome fairies dressed in grey used to haunt the countryside round Pentrefoelas.

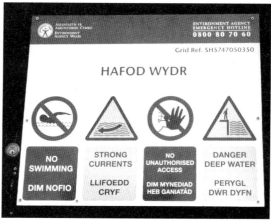

33. The pool known as the 'Lake of the Maiden's Cries' is haunted by the spirit of an unfortunate girl who drowned in it. The pool is now so overgrown as to be impossible to photograph but this sign on a water board hut nearby shows that its waters are still treacherous.

34. The barren peak of Bron Bannog, a mountain rich in fairy-lore

35. The 'Fairy House' found by Judy Young in a remote wood in the area of Bron Bannog (see plate 34). This strange, intricate little wigwam has defied explanation, and Judy was never able to find it again. Picture: Judy Young

followed, singing from tree to tree, right to his door . . .

The cuckoo, featured as something rather unearthly in Welsh folklore (see also page 156). This very weird story also hints at a belief among rural folk that spirits could somehow control their fate or that of their community. In some Welsh villages it was believed that at Hallowe'en an invisible spirit would occupy the church and, at midnight, name all the people who were to die in the parish during the following twelve months.

At the little village of Llangernyw, in Conwy, this grim spirit was known as the Angel-ystor. One fateful Hallowe'en night a tailor, who fancied himself as a bit of a wit, drunkenly announced that he was going to prove that Angel-ystor was a myth. Ignoring the warnings of his friends, the tailor, whose name was Siôn Robert, left the pub and weaved his inebriated way to the church. Smirking, he cocked his ear to the east window and promptly heard a grim and sonorous voice announce: 'Siôn ap Robert!' Siôn's heart was clutched with fear and he blurted out: 'Hold! Hold! I am not quite ready.'

But, ready or not, Siôn Robert died that year.

At Llantysilio, near Llangollen, a man was summoned out of his bed by a spirit and he followed it all the way to the isolated little church perched high above the River Dee. Although it was midnight, he found the church illuminated and he could hear voices inside. These voices – presumably those of spirits – pronounced doom on the local squire. They said he would soon die an unnatural death and a stranger would take over Llantysilio Hall.

This is exactly what happened. The squire died of a

septic finger he cut on a broken wine bottle and a stranger barricaded himself into the Hall during the squire's funeral, claiming he had won it in a gambling debt.

Such stories suggest something like the sort of ancestor worship still practised by various cultures around the world. It is almost as if these spirits were those of the long dead, keeping a watch over the doings of their descendants in their communities.

There is a strong link between spirits of the dead and the fairies. Fairies were believed to live beneath the waters of many Welsh lakes (see, for example, page 78), just as the spirits of Flint Mountain lived beneath the Pwll-y-Wrach. Perhaps these spirits and the fairies were the same.

(Pwll-y-Wrach is quite difficult to find. For those keen to seek it out, it can be found using the Ordnance Survey Explorer map 265, at grid reference 234703.)

Sources: *Howell Gwynedd* by G. Bellys, *Welsh Folklore* by Elias Owen; the 1892 volume of *Bye-gones*. See plates 14 and 15.

Fairies

Do you believe in fairies?

'I do believe in fairies – I do, I do!' Such is the chant taken up in the latest film version of J.M. Barrie's *Peter Pan*.

It is not an admission one is likely to hear much today. However, strange though it might seem, fairies and goblins have been reported in Wales in recent times.

One day in 1961, a perfectly ordinary, normally unimaginative gentleman (who does not wish to be named) was walking his dog down a country lane called Coed Esgob, near St Asaph. Part of the way along this lane there is a white metal post, which was once the base for a way-sign. The man paused here for a moment and tapped his walking stick against the post several times to knock the mud off it.

As if summoned by the tapping, a horrible little man suddenly appeared. He was only three foot tall, was dressed all in green and had an ugly brown face. He glared malevolently at the astonished man, who felt rooted to the spot. His dog growled and raised its hackles at the glowering goblin – who vanished as suddenly as he had come.

This entity sounds a bit like the 'little old fellow' seen by a Mr Jones at Llanystumdwy in Eifionydd, but that was back in the 1920s. Mr Jones told folklorist Robin Gwyndaf that when he was out collecting firewood as a boy, he saw a man just three foot tall emerge from some bushes. The figure wore green from the waist down and had a little red cap on his head.

In the 1960s, a botanist camping out on Mynydd Llangynidr, near Brecon, saw 'hordes of tiny people' playing about the spot where he was collecting plants. A local farmer later told him that the name of the place where he saw them translated as 'Fairies' Bog'.

Perhaps the weirdest recent encounter with little people recorded from Wales took place in Swansea. In 1972 a woman told *The Sun* newspaper the following extraordinary story:

'When my sons were small and sleeping in our back room, they were woken up by a dwarf-like figure with a huge face. He pulled their hair, ran around and made a getaway through the window. He never woke them both up. It was one boy one night and the other the next. They were never hurt and said the dwarf wanted to play and got annoyed if they wanted to sleep.'

Evidently, belief in fairies and goblins is very much alive.

Sources: The Coed Esgob story was told to me by a friend of the witness; the next two stories also appear in *Fairies: Encounters With Little People* by Janet Bord; the Swansea story was originally in *The Sun*, then reprinted in volume 7 of *The News*. Scc plate 8.

At home with the fairies?

One day Judy Young and some friends were walking in a remote and rather wild forest on the borders of Conwy and Denbighshire, when they stumbled – almost literally – on something very strange indeed.

In the depths of the wood, nestling under a conifer, was a tiny, intricately made structure composed of leaves, pine needles and twigs. It was a kind of wigwam, corralled within a delicate fence, but only big enough for a mouse or a sparrow to live in. Or a fairy.

The area where the tiny house was found – a few miles south of the Alwen Reservoir – is rich in fairylore. Many of the legends collected by the Victorian folklorist Elias Owen were set very near where the house was found, but this was unknown to Judy at the time. However, it was immediately picked up on by her friend, the Denbighshire writer Janet Bord, when she was shown a picture of the 'house'. The photograph is one of the many intriguing entries in Janet Bord's book *The Traveller's Guide to Fairy Sites* (Gothic Image Publications).

Fairy Sites is a superbly researched and very readable gazetteer of locations throughout England, Scotland and Wales where fairies are said to have appeared. Wales is particularly well represented because, of course, Janet lives here, and the book includes many fascinating and beautiful places to visit in the local area.

Unfortunately, one is unable to visit the 'fairy house', for it has vanished – Judy, who lives on the Hiraethog and walks in that isolated forest a great deal, has never seen it again nor anything remotely like it. But what was it?

'Obviously one's common sense tells one that it must have been made by a human . . . but why?' pondered Janet Bord in an e-mail to me. 'They would not expect it to be found, or seen, by anyone, as it was definitely off the beaten track. All I can think is that it was made by a practitioner of some nature religion, in homage to . . . what or who?' No good explanation ever presented itself as to what this strange structure could have been. One idea that it might have been a shrine for a dead pet was dismissed both for its isolation and the fact that the ground around it was in no way disturbed.

The finding of the 'fairy house' is perhaps further evidence of the magical beliefs that still survive in Wales. As already indicated, fairy sightings are not necessarily things of the past.

Source: *The Traveller's Guide to Fairy Sites* by Janet Bord with special thanks to Judy Young. See plate 35.

Around Bron Bannog

The region of countryside in which the 'Fairy House' was found is particularly rich in tales of the Tylwyth Teg *(fair people)*, which is one of the reasons why Janet Bord and I were so intrigued by its discovery.

Elias Owen collected many stories from this wild bit of country, which consists mainly of open moorland and some Forestry Commission plantations, dominated by the peak of Bron Bannog. The Ychen Bannog, gigantic mythical oxen, appear to have been named after this mountain, and it is an interesting fact that it is crowned by two tor-like outcrops of rock which, at certain angles, resemble the horns of a bull.

The Ychen Bannog were the offspring of a fairy cow called the Fuwch Frech *(freckled cow)*, who had her home among the ruins of ancient habitations now swallowed up by the forest of Clocaenog. A Mr Thomas Jones, of Cefn Bannog Farm, told Elias Owen a version of the legend of the Fuwch Frech in the 1880s, one which 'the old people have transmitted from generation to generation'. He reported:

'Whenever anyone was in want of milk they went to this cow, taking with them a vessel into which they milked the cow, and, however big this vessel was, they always departed with the pail filled with rich milk, and it made no difference, however often she was milked, she could never be milked dry. This continued for a long time, and glad indeed the people were to avail themselves of the inexhaustible supply of new milk, freely given to all.

'At last a wicked hag, filled with envy at the people's prosperity, determined to milk the cow dry, and for this purpose she took a riddle with her, and milked and milked the cow, until at last she could get no more milk from her. But, sad to say, the cow immediately, upon this treatment, left the country, and was never more seen.'

Another version of the tale further states that the Fuwch Frech went to a lake about four miles away and, bellowing piteously, disappeared beneath its waters. The Ychen Bannog followed her, entering the lake, one on each side, and they too were never seen again. Ever afterwards the lake was known by the name of Llyn Dau Ychen (*Dau Ychen*: two oxen).

Llyn Dau Ychen has silted up over the years and is now a marsh on the edge of the Alwen reservoir. It was very near here that Judy Young found her 'Fairy House'.

The farmer, Thomas Jones, told Owen that fairies had been seen in the neighbourhood, 'but not often now'. Owen continues: 'Jones said that some children had seen them on the hill close by. The day was misty and the clouds capped the hills, and the children saw a large number of diminutive folk, dressed in blue, emerging from the clouds, and then rushing back into the clouds.'

This singular account suggests the UFO aspects of some fairylore, further discussed on pages 82 and 83. The grandmother of one of Mr Thomas's neighbours reputedly got on very well with the local fairies. This lady – Owen refers to her as 'Mrs R.' – was referred to by the friendly Tylwyth Teg as 'Aunty Ann' and she in turn got to know each of them by name. When she was gathering rushes at Pont Petrual – a very pretty place popular with walkers today – the fairies' dog would run up to greet her, 'just as any other dog would come to welcome its master's friend'.

Adds Owen:'It was very evident that the fairy tribe loved Mrs R. and that she loved them.'

Source: *Welsh Folklore* by Elias Owen; the 1886 volume of *Archaeologia Cambrensis*. See plate 34.

Village fays

Not so many miles away from fairy-haunted Hiraethog, on the borders of Snowdonia National Park, there is a village which also seems to have been a popular abode of the fairies – Pentrefoelas, in Conwy.

In the late nineteenth century the vicar of Pentrefoelas was the Rev. Owen Jones, a good friend of the Rev. Elias Owen, who was busy collecting tales for what became his book of *Welsh Folklore*. Mr Jones was enthusiastic about the folklore and stories of his own parish and passed on the many stories he heard to Owen, of which the following is a good example:

'A Pentrefoelas man was coming home one lovely summer's night, and when within a stone's throw of his house, he heard in the far distance singing of the most enchanting kind. He stopped to listen to the sweet sounds which filled him with a sensation of deep pleasure.

'He had not listened long ere he perceived that the singers were approaching. By and by they came to the spot where he was, and he saw that they were marching in single file and consisted of a number of small people, robed in close-fitting grey clothes, and they were accompanied by speckled dogs that marched along two deep like soldiers.

'When the procession came quite opposite the enraptured listener, it stopped, and the small people spoke to him and earnestly begged him to accompany them, but he would not. They tried many ways, and for a long time, to persuade him to join them, but when they saw they could not induce him to do so they departed, dividing themselves into two companies and marching away, the dogs marching two abreast in front of each company. They sang as they went away the most entrancing music that was ever heard.

'The man, spell-bound, stood where he was, listening to the ravishing music of the fairies, and he did not enter his house until the last sound had died away in the far-off distance.'

This man's extraordinary vision was far from the only encounter with fairies to be had by the folk of Pentrefoelas. A very hardworking, tidy lady of the village, the sort of woman who 'had a place for everything, and kept everything in its place', made sure she carried out her tasks before retiring to bed. She would sweep the hearth, brush up the ashes and leave a few fresh peats on the fire to keep the cottage warm. The fairies were attracted to the clean and tidy cottage and spent many a night enjoying themselves there. To say thank you, they always left a bright, shiny shilling behind for the woman to find in the morning. One day, the woman's neighbours, envious of her prosperity and noticing that she always paid for her goods with a new coin, asked where she got it from – and in her simplicity, she told them. But, alas, the fairies were offended at her for divulging their secret, and afterwards they never came to her home, and there were no more shiny shillings to be found in the morning.

One had to treat the fairies with respect – they would repay kindnesses done to them, but could be tricky, as shown in this story:

'One day when she was returning from Pentrefoelas Church, the wife of Hafod y Garreg found on the ground in an exhausted state a fairy dog. She took it up tenderly and carried it home in her apron. She showed this kindness to the poor little thing from fear, for she remembered what had happened to the wife of Bryn Heilyn, who had found one of the Fairy dogs, but had behaved cruelly towards it, and consequently had fallen down dead. The wife of Hafod y Garreg, therefore, made a nice soft bed for the fairy dog in the pantry, and placed over it a brass pot.

'In the night succeeding the day that she had found the dog, a company of fairies came to Hafod y Garreg to make inquiries after it. The woman told them that it was safe and sound, and that they were welcome to take it away with them. She willingly gave it up to its masters. Her conduct pleased the fairies greatly, and so, before departing with the dog, they asked her which she would prefer, a clean or dirty cow? Her answer was: 'A dirty one'.

'And so it came to pass that from that time forward to the end of her life, her cows gave more milk than the very best cows, in the very best farms in her neighbourhood. In this way was she rewarded for her kindness to the dog by the fairies.'

The next time you are travelling on the A5 into Snowdonia, pause at Pentrefoelas and take the time to potter about. It's a magical place.

Source: *Welsh Folklore* by Elias Owen. See plate 32.

Surf and turf

There are many pools and lakes with strange legends attached to them in the midst of Snowdonia.

One whose legend was recorded very early on is Llyn Dywarchen in the romantic Nantlle Valley. The name means 'Lake of the Turf Sod'. The Welsh historian Giraldus Cambrensis was writing about it as long ago as the twelfth century. He claimed the lake had 'a floating island driven from one side to the other by the wind'. This unique feature could prove troublesome to the local farmers because on occasions they would have to watch 'their cattle, while feeding, driven to distant parts of the lake'.

The phenomenon of the floating isle was still being witnessed as late as the eighteenth century. One chap, by the name of Holly, claimed he swam out to the island and steered it round the lake.

It is possible the soil around the lake was so peaty that chunks could become detached and float as described, but there is no way now of knowing what the truth might be, because Llyn y Dywarchen, in common with many other lakes in Snowdonia, has been converted into a reservoir. The island which can still be seen in the water is solid rock – and quite immovable.

The floating island is not the only legendary aspect of Llyn y Dywarchen. It was also once the haunt of fairies. One moonlit night a young man was passing the lake when he saw a party of fairy maidens dancing near its shores. One in particular 'whose appearance was like alabaster' caught his fancy and he boldly rushed down on the dancers and snatched her up in her arms and carried her away. Her name was Penelop, and after much protestation, she at length agreed to marry the youth. There was one condition, however: that he should never strike her with iron – which seemed to her new husband an unlikely occurrence.

They lived together contentedly for many years and the fairy girl bore the mortal man two children, a boy and a girl. One fateful day, the man decided to catch a filly grazing in his field so that he could sell it at Caernarfon market. The animal kept eluding him and at last he asked his wife to help him. Alas! When he made another attempt to bridle the horse, the bridle struck his wife instead – and the condition of the marriage was at that moment broken, for she had been struck with iron. The fairy woman instantly vanished.

The poor fellow never saw her again. But one frosty night, years later, he heard her voice below his window and they had a brief conversation. He learnt that she had returned to dwell under the waters of Llyn y Dywarchen.

Sources: *A Description of Wales* by Giraldus Cambrensis; *Celtic Folklore* by John Rhys. See plate 16.

Home help

Few people enjoy housework. In the old days the gentry had servants to do all the boring, dirty chores for them, but even the poor folk of Wales sometimes found some help, but from a very unexpected source. Occasionally a humble Welsh cottage would find itself with a strange lodger – a lodger who did all the housework.

These 'lodgers' were rarely seen; usually they were invisible, and all one would know of their presence was the results of their labours – the hearth would be swept, the dishes washed and stacked, the butter churned. Usually this was done overnight while the household slept.

These friendly poltergeists went by a number of names. Sometimes they were referred to as a Pwca, sometimes as a Bwbach, although the latter word was also used to describe an especially scary ghost.

The most famous Pwca was the Pwca'r Trwyn who haunted a farm of that name in south Wales in about the year 1700. This Pwca was never seen but was often heard, and was more than a little cheeky. After knocking boldly on the farm door, and terrifying everybody by greeting them invisibly out of the darkness, he set up home in the oven, from where he would often chat to the family.

It was customary to pay helpful spirits like the Pwca'r Trwyn with a bowl of cream, or cream and bread, which would be left for it in the kitchen by the maid or by the lady of the house before she retired for the night.

Such a gift was welcome, but it was a mistake to be too generous. People who were lucky enough to actually catch a glimpse of their Pwca were always moved to pity by the sight – for, in contrast to the heavy labours he undertook, they would see that he was very small and frail-looking, and also naked. It was the nakedness which most upset the ladies of the house and they would immediately set about making a little suit of clothes for their helper. Once made, they would lay the clothes out with the cream.

But if they expected thanks, they were much mistaken. Either the Pwca would be deeply offended by the gift, or he would put it on and dance about in high spirits but in either case the result would be the same. The Pwca would leave that night, never to return.

J.K. Rowling used this bit of folklore in her Harry Potter books. A gift of clothing was all that was needed to free Dobby the House Elf. However, his first act on getting his freedom was to zap his former master with a nasty spell. This, at least, was spared the good wives of Wales – the worst they had to contend with on their Pwca's retirement was a pile of dirty dishes.

Source: *Apparitions of Spirits* by Edmund Jones; *British Goblins* by Wirt Sikes.

Fairies from space

There are many intriguing parallels between the old belief in fairies and the modern day belief in aliens and UFOs.

Take the following story, for example. The action takes place in the neighbourhood of Portmeirion on a dark night one year in the first half of the nineteenth century – more than a century before the concept of a UFO was even conceived.

A young woman named Miss Jones was walking home from a neighbour's house and she had with her a servant known by the nickname of Dafydd Fawr ('Big David') 'because of his great strength and stature'. Dafydd was carrying a joint of bacon on his back and was walking rather slowly. Miss Jones hurried on her way through the night, as Dafydd followed.

When she arrived home, however, Miss Jones was surprised to find that Dafydd was not with her – and it was another three hours before he finally turned up, the bacon still on his back. The servant was amazed when he was told how late it was. He was sure he had been just a few minutes behind Miss Jones, but he explained he had been briefly delayed by a strange sight, which was reported as follows:

'He observed, he said, a brilliant meteor passing through the air, which was followed by a ring or hoop of fire, and within this hoop stood a man and woman of small size, handsomely dressed. With one arm they embraced each other, and with the other they took hold of the hoop, and their feet rested on the concave surface of the ring.

'When the hoop reached the earth these two beings jumped out of it, and immediately proceeded to make a circle upon the ground. As soon as this was done, a large number of men and women instantly appeared, and to the sweetest music that ear ever heard commenced dancing round and round the circle.

'The sight was so entrancing that the man stayed, as he thought a few minutes, to witness the scene. The ground all around was lit up by a kind of subdued light, and he observed every movement of these beings.

'By and by the meteor which had at first attracted his attention appeared again, and then the fiery hoop came to view, and when it reached the spot where the dancing was, the lady and gentleman who had arrived in it jumped into the hoop, and disappeared in the same manner in which they had reached the place.

'Immediately after their departure the fairies vanished from sight, and the man found himself alone and in darkness, and then proceeded homewards. For this reason he accounted for his delay on the way.'

The 'meteor' and the strange beings arriving to earth in a glowing circular object are clearly similar to UFO stories. It is also significant that the experience of 'missing time' – hours or even days or years passing by in what seems but a few minutes – is equally common in fairylore as it is in accounts of alien abduction.

This poses the question – were fairies the aliens of our forefathers?

Source: *Welsh Folklore* by Elias Owen.

Changelings

One night a couple took their beloved baby out of its bed and carried it to a big tree which grew near their cottage. They put it under the tree and then walked home. Their poor baby was left out in the cold all night.

This seemingly cruel act was actually carried out through love – and an old folk belief. The infant had been so peevish that its parents began to believe it was not their baby at all, that it was an impostor – a changeling.

Belief in changelings was once widespread in Wales. It was believed that the fairies coveted human babies and would steal them when they could. The stolen baby would be substituted by a fairy baby whose peevishness and ugliness would often give him away.

The incident above took place near Holywell in Flintshire and it was recorded by Thomas Pennant, a celebrated traveller and antiquarian, in his book *A History of Whiteford and Holywell*, which was published in 1796. The tree where the child was left was not chosen at random – it was known as the Fairy Oak, and grew on a mound behind Pennant's home, Downing Hall.

The cottagers believed that although fairies liked to steal human children, they could not bear any harm coming to their own. By leaving the supposed changeling out all night under the Fairy Oak, they believed the fairies would know the game was up and rather than allow their own baby to suffer, would retrieve it and return the human one.

Fortunately, the infant was unharmed by its ordeal and the next morning its parents took it home, convinced they had done the right thing. The baby was lucky – there are tales of mothers dangling small children off bridges in the hope the fairies would come for it. The treatment of 'changelings' adds a sinister aspect to this particular belief.

Edmund Jones, a preacher who lived in Monmouthshire in the eighteenth century, is one of our earliest sources for Welsh fairylore. He was firmly convinced of the existence of fairies, claiming to have seen them himself, and he also believed in changelings. He describes the son of a neighbour of his, a Mr Edmund John William, who was supposed to have been changed by the fairies, 'leaving an idiot in his stead'.

Of the boy Jones writes: 'I saw him myself; there was something diabolical in his aspect, but more of this in his motion and voice – for his motions were mad and he made very disagreeable screaming sounds which frightened some strangers who passed by. His complexion was a dark, tawny colour.'

It is possible many disabled children, perhaps autistic or with Down's Syndrome, were once presumed to be changelings. The treatment they suffered as a result hardly bears thinking about, but is chillingly suggested by an unfeeling Edmund Jones in regards to this unfortunate child about whom he observes:

'He lived longer than such children used to live, until he was (I think) ten or twelve years of age.'

Sources: *History of Whiteford and Holywell* by Thomas Pennant; *Apparitions of Spirits* by Edmund Jones.

The Green Meadows of Enchantment

On uncomfortably hot, humid days in summer how nice it would be to escape from the office and find oneself in the Green Meadows of Enchantment. The Gwerddonau Llion, or Green Meadows, were said to exist just below the surface of the sea, occasionally rising to the surface when their inhabitants wished to come ashore. The land was a very pleasant place which few mortals were ever allowed to visit.

Old tales tell of a piece of land between Aberdaron in Llŷn and northern Pembrokeshire which was invisible to ordinary eyes. This watery world was the home of a tribe of people called the Plant Rhys Ddwfn which fairy expert Katherine Briggs translates as 'The Family of Rhys the Deep-Minded'.

These people, who were rather smaller than humans but very good-looking, had lived in the Land of Rhys for countless generations. They would come ashore to buy from local markets and appreciated fair dealing and honesty. One merchant whom they trusted was one Gruffydd ab Einion and he was once invited to visit the Plant Rhys Ddwfn on their island.

Gruffydd was mysteriously transported there, and found that it was a land filled with treasures, which the fairies – for such they were – had gathered from all over the world, showing that they were great traders. He went home laden with costly gifts, and because he never betrayed the Rhysians, he remained on good terms with them for the rest of his life.

Perhaps belief in the Green Meadows of Enchantment

was not all fantasy. In 1896 a Captain Jones told a Welsh newspaper that when his ship was passing Ynys Gwales *(Grassholm Island)* off the coast of Pembrokeshire in the Celtic Sea, he was surprised to see: 'A large tract of land covered with a beautiful green meadow. It was not, however, above water, but just a few feet below, say two or three, so that the grass waved and swam about as the ripple flowed over it, in a most delightful way to the eye, so that watching it made one feel quite drowsy.'

He continued: 'I have heard old people say there is a floating island off there, that sometimes rises to the surface, or nearly, and when nobody expects, it comes up again for a while. How it may be I do not know, but that is what they say.'

Perhaps the Green Meadows of Enchantment are there still, so close and yet so far out of reach.

Sources: *Cambrian Superstitions* by William Howells; *British Goblins* by Wirt Sikes; *Celtic Folklore* by John Rhys; *The Vanishing People* by Katherine Briggs.

A mermaid

Early one morning in the summer of 1826 a Ceredigion farmer went down to the rocks at the end of his field to take a look at the sea. Imagine his embarrassment when he saw, just a stone's throw away, a beautiful young woman washing herself in the waves.

Blushing, the farmer turned away. Then he realised there was something rather odd – the tide was in and the woman was comfortably bobbing about in at least six feet of water. So he threw himself down on a rock and allowed himself a good look. Then he went and fetched his family.

Altogether twelve people trooped out of the farm, including children and servants, and they all threw themselves down on the ground so that the strange and lovely young woman couldn't see them. All that is, except for the farmer's wife – perhaps she found this mass vouyeurism distasteful. She strode boldly up in full view, and the mysterious woman immediately stopped her ablutions and dived into the sea.

She swam a little further off and whole family followed her progress by running along the shore. Often she could be seen bending down 'as if taking up water' and as she did this what did they catch a glimpse of? Yes, a tail! Of course, the woman was a mermaid.

Mermaid sightings are rare in Wales. This one, which took place about three miles from Aberystwyth, is one of the very few. There is a story of a mermaid caught in a net further down the Ceredigion coastline at Llannarth, and another of a mermaid befriending a fisherman in Pembrokeshire, but that's about it.

The Aberystwyth story is the best, because the account of her was taken from the family a few years after they had seen her. She was certainly a beauty:

'She was exactly the same as a young woman of about eighteen years of age. Her hair was short, and of a dark colour; her face rather handsome, her neck and arms like those of any ordinary woman, her breast blameless and her skin whiter than that of any person they had ever seen before.'

She seemed to take no further notice of the curious onlookers and never uttered a word. The only sound she made was 'some noise like sneezing'. Well, anyone in the habit of 'taking up water' might sneeze, too.

Source: *Folklore of West and Mid Wales* by J. Ceredig Davies.

Monsters

Here be dragons

Snowdonia is a region of great mystery as well as spectacular scenery, and its ancient hills hold many secrets.

Near Beddgelert there rises a craggy, wooded hill named Dinas Emrys. On its summit there can be found the remains of a Dark Age fortress, which tradition credits as the retreat of the Welsh king Vortigern. He was the man who foolishly invited Saxon mercenaries to his country, which resulted in them deciding to stay . . .

There is a famous legend attached to these ruins, a legend at the heart of the national identity of Wales. It is said that when Vortigern attempted to build his fortress, he was frustrated by inexplicable earth tremors that caused the walls to tumble down before it could be completed. He was advised to seek out a youth without a father, for such a boy – if he existed – would have the power of divination, and would be able to explain the cause of the disturbances.

Such a boy was found, a boy who had been fathered not by a man but by a demon. His name was Myrddin – known in English as Merlin.

Myrddin's power of second sight enabled him to see that below the foundations of Vortigern's fort there was a huge cave containing a subterranean lake. In this lake there were two dragons. One was red and one was white and they were locked together in mortal combat, their struggles shaking the mountain.

Myrddin explained that the dragons were symbols – the Red Dragon represented Wales and the White represented the Saxon invaders. Using his magic, Myrddin quelled the warring monsters and then created a magnificent fortress for Vortigern to use.

Ever since that day, the Red Dragon, or Ddraig Goch, has been the badge of the Cymro.

If we are to believe the old legends, Wales was once crawling with dragons – fearsome reptilian beasts, often winged, which would devour people and animals with equal gusto.

One such monster once made its nest in the ruins of Denbigh castle. The story is set in the sixteenth century: the hero credited with dispatching the dragon was one Sir John Salusbury – a real historical figure.

Sir John is said to have been a giant of a man who had the added advantage of double the usual number of fingers and thumbs on each hand, and was known therefore as Sir John of the Thumbs. This proved thumbs up for the people of Denbigh and a thumbs down for the dragon – because, after a fierce fight, Sir John was able to cut off its head.

Another dragon – known as the Wybr, or Viper – had its lair near the highest waterfall in Wales, Pistyll Rhaeadr, near Llanrhaeadr-ym-Mochnant in northern Powys, which has a drop of two hundred and forty feet and is one of the most beautiful waterfalls in Britain. Situated at the end of a lovely and isolated valley, the Afon Rhaeadr plunges down a sheer cliff in a white cascade, thundering under a romantic arch of stone before babbling away through a pine forest. It is a peaceful, indeed mystical, place.

One writer states that the waterfall itself was the Wybr's lair. The monster slept by day behind the impenetrable curtain of water, but at night it would unfurl its bat-like wings and then swoop off across the Berwyn mountains, snapping up any stray animals and children it could find. It was a terror to the neighbourhood and the people began to despair. They did not have a hero to call on like the lucky folk of Denbigh but fortunately, a wise man (a 'Dyn Hysbys' in Welsh) lived in the neighbourhood and he told them what to do.

He had the people erect a great pillar of stone and into this he directed them to drive sharpened iron spikes. This gigantic mace was then draped in red cloth and a fire lit under it at sunset to attract the dragon's attention.

The stupid dragon apparently imagined that the fiery red pillar was a rival, so, like an overgrown budgie in front of a mirror, it attacked it. The hidden spikes pierced its leathery skin, but this only enraged it further, and it continued to hurl itself onto the stone until it had torn itself to ribbons. So ended the dragon of Pistyll Rhaeadr.

The pillar still stands. It is a massive standing stone known by the name of the Post Coch *(red pillar)*, and can be found in a field a few miles east of Llanrhaeadr. It is the tallest prehistoric standing stone in Wales.

It is possible that these tales of savage scaly brutes are based on a real animal, now extinct, although it seems unlikely. But what is to be made of the report of a giant reptile encountered at Overton-on-Dee, near Wrexham, in the nineteenth century?

According to *Overton in Days Gone By*, published in 1883, a 'huge snake' leapt out of a hedge near Overton Bridge and attacked a team of horses carrying a cart of coal. With great difficulty the wagoner fought the thing off and succeeded in killing it. The snake's carcass was so long that when he draped it over his cart, its head reached the ground in front and its tail dragged along behind . . .

Sources: *Folklore and Folk Custom* by T. Gwynn Jones; *Folk-Lore and Folk Stories of Wales* by Marie Trevelyan; *Prehistoric and Roman Remains in Denbighshire* by Ellis Davies; *Tales of Northern Wales* by Ken Radford; *Overton in Days Gone By by* G.J. Howson. See plates 17 and 18.

The lurker in the lake

As anglers, windsurfers and sailors flock to Llyn Tegid every summer, they are aware that something very big and very nasty could be lurking beneath the waves. Llyn Tegid is Wales's very own Loch Ness, for it too is said to have a monster.

Llyn Tegid, known to tourists as Bala Lake, is three-and-a-half miles long, an average of half a mile wide and is fifty feet deep – a lot of water to hide a monster. The river Dee runs into Llyn Tegid at its northern end and back out again in the south, and five other streams also empty into it, providing plenty of places where something could get in and out of the lake.

Rumours about a monster in Llyn Tegid began in the 1970s and for a long while I assumed the whole thing was a joke. But some years ago I spoke to a very serious and sober angler of great experience who, in the company of three others, had seen something inexplicable in the lake.

He told me:'We were standing on the road leading down to the lake when suddenly we saw a big boil of water, twenty to twenty-five feet across. At first we thought a windsurfer had come to grief or something like that but then we saw a dark object swirl around in the middle of the disturbance. It began to move upwind, leaving a wake behind it.

'It moved much faster than a big shoal of fish, and no shoal of fish could push the water like this thing was. I have fished Llyn Tegid for twenty years and I have never seen anything like it.'

The warden told me that he had not seen anything

himself but had spoken to many people who claimed to have seen 'a dark shape moving at tremendous speed just under the water'. The reports he had received tended to make him think that it might be 'crocodile-like'.

These modern accounts of a monster – it has already been christened 'Teggy' – are not the first hint that something big and nasty is lurking in the lake. In 1909, Marie Trevelyan, describing attempts to measure the depth of Llyn Tegid, wrote: 'Centuries ago an expert diver tried it, but was terribly frightened by his experience. He asserted that a dragon was coiled up at the bottom of the lake, and if he had not been very careful the creature would have swallowed him.'

The ancient Welsh Triads also speak of a horrible lake monster, the Afanc, inhabiting a lake called Llyn Llion. The beast used to make the waters of the Lake of Waves overflow. After the first inundation, only two people survived – Dwyfan and Dwyfach. Interestingly enough, Dwyfan and Dwyfach are the names of two streams which run into Llyn Tegid – so Llyn Tegid could be the Llyn Llion mentioned in the Triads.

The Afanc of Llyn Llion was dragged out of the lake by a might hero, Hu Gadarn, and King Arthur similarly defeated a monster which inhabited Llyn Barfog, near Aberdyfi. A pool in the river Conwy near Betws-y-coed also possessed an Afanc. By means of a cunning woman, who helped tame the fearsome beast, the Afanc was wrapped in chains and dragged out of its pool and over the mountains to Llyn Ffynnon Las in the neighbourhood of Beddgelert. Here the Afanc was allowed to live, for Llyn Ffynnon Las was so isolated that it was no longer a trouble to people. Any sheep or goats that strayed too close to the water's edge were immediately pulled under and devoured, however.

So what was the Afanc? The word means 'beaver' in Welsh and the beaver did live in certain parts of Wales as late as the Middle Ages. But it would have to have been an enormous beaver to devour men or sheep. Like the dragon, some have speculated that the Afanc was some sort of prehistoric monster, now extinct.

Source: Personal communication with the author; *Welsh Folk-Lore and Folk-Stories* by Marie Trevelyan; *Welsh Folklore and Folk Custom* by T. Gwynn Jones, and *Beddgelert: Its Facts, Fairies and Folklore by* D.E. Jenkins. See plate 23.

Serpent ahoy!

If a stretch of water the size of Llyn Tegid could contain a monster, then what about the waters around the country? The sea may be full of monsters.

If you find that hard to credit, take as an example this account of a sea serpent which attacked a ship in the Menai Strait:'Once in October, in the year 1805, as a small vessel of the Traeth was upon the Menai, sailing very slowly, the weather being very calm, the people on board saw a strange creature like an immense worm swimming after them.

'It soon overtook them, climbed on board through the tiller-hole, and coiled itself on the deck under the mast – the people at first were dreadfully frightened, but taking courage they attacked it with an oar and drove it overboard; it followed the vessel for some time, but a breeze springing up, they lost sight of it.'

This adventure was recounted by George Borrow in his famous book *Wild Wales*. He had read it in a very old Welsh periodical *Y Greal (The Grail)* and repeated it to a party of sceptical seafaring men in a pub at Y Felinheli.

Although the sailors themselves did not believe in sea serpents, one did remember the story Borrow told them and recalled that the name of the ship attacked by the monster was the *Robert Ellis*.

The Menai monster is not the only sea serpent to have invaded the waters of the Welsh coast. In September 1882 several witnesses saw a serpent swimming towards the Great Orme at Llandudno. This one was enormous – estimated at two hundred feet in length. It moved faster than most sailing vessels and swam in a strange corkscrew motion.

In 1975 there was a positive swarm of sea monsters. On March 2nd of that year six schoolgirls, all aged twelve, were startled by something 'horrible' they saw on Llanaber beach about two hundred yards away from where they stood. 'It was like a dinosaur,' said one of the girls. 'The monster was about ten feet long, with a long tail, long neck and huge green eyes. It walked towards the sea and entered the water.'

The creature's green eyes peered at them before sinking beneath the waves. The girls, not surprisingly, ran away in terror. On hearing of the sighting, an oceanography expert from Menai Bridge kindly suggested the girls had seen an otter, or perhaps a seal, and that a trick of the light had confused them as to its size. He added: 'No known creature that could have escaped from tropical waters would fit the girls' description.'

The whole thing might be a childish fantasy, but reports of other ocean-going monsters were being reported at about the same time. Several people saw a large creature moving at speed into Red Wharf Bay on Anglesey. A barman at the local hotel described it as being blackish in colour and about twelve feet long, including a rather prominent tail. He said: 'It was too weird and rather frightening to be a basking shark, a dolphin or even a miniature submarine. It resembled a flying bomb from its tail and we saw it before hearing about this Barmouth monster.'

Following this revelation, reports of similar beasts appeared in the northern Wales press – including something swimming in the Mawddach estuary, 'six young monsters' found dead on the beach at Tal-y-bont, and a 'weird, crocodile-like creature walking along a riverbank near Harlech'.

As recently as 2003, a sea serpent was reported swimming into Milford Haven harbour in Pembrokeshire. It was described as being 'dark and snake-like and roughly the length of four or five cars'. It thrashed away in the water just ten metres away from astonished drinkers at a seaside pub. Then with a flick of its tail, it vanished below the waves.

Perhaps our waters are not as safe as we thought?

Sources: *Wild Wales* by George Borrow; contemporary accounts collected in volumes 10 and 11 of *The News; Western Telegraph* for March 12, 2003. See plate 19.

Crocodile cave

Cefn Caves, near St Asaph, are extensive caverns once occupied by prehistoric man. They have revealed many surprises, not least of which is the oldest human remain found in Britain – an ancient tooth.

But even this does not compare with what *The Times* said in 1870 was found in the caves – a crocodile.

'It had been rumoured of late that parties visiting this place had on several occasions seen some dark animal creeping in its dark recesses,' wrote *The Times* reporter on the 20th of October that year, 'and on Saturday visitors reported having had a good view of him, and stated it was a huge beast of the lizard tribe.

'On the Monday following, Thomas Hughes, from Rhyl, went to try and capture him. Armed with a stout stick, he approached its reported lair, but not seeing it he decided to remain in ambush at the mouth of the cave, sheltered by a projecting ledge. After having thus waited an hour this patience was rewarded with success.

'He could hear in the far end a hum as in a hive of bees. The sound growing louder, and now apparently quite close, Hughes peeped round the ledge and saw the monster within three yards of him.

'He sprang towards him, and dextrously wielding his stick he dealt him a well-aimed blow upon the neck just behind the head, which caused him to stagger and reel. One more blow in the abdomen finished him.

'Hughes carried him home in triumph, and is now making a profit out of the affair by exhibiting him in Rhyl. The monster is of the lizard tribe, as mentioned above. Only that our country is destitute in these creatures, we should have said it was a young crocodile.'

I repeated this story in the *Wales of the Unexpected* column on April the 1st, 2004 – a suitable day because, of course, it was all a hoax. Writer Michael Goss unearthed the original newspaper report and reprinted it in *Fortean Times*, where he pointed out that the *Times* reporter must have known the tale was a put-on because of his reference to the 'hum as in a hive of bees' – he was hinting to his readers that it was all 'humbug'.

The lizard had, in fact, been long dead when Thomas Hughes acquired it from a travelling showman. Hughes sold it on to another man for sixpence, and was then talked into 'finding' and 'killing' the beast so that the pair of them could exhibit it – charging tuppence a head!

Blood suckers

Dragons, afancs, sea-serpents – Wales has its fair share of monster stories, but it also has its stories about the most famous monster of them all, the vampire. In 1890, a French newspaper told its readers about a Vampire of Snowdon. The article reported:

'There exists in north Wales a legend according to which an extraordinary being which passes for a vampire formerly haunted the recesses of Snowdon. If unfortunately any young people ventured near his retreat he threw himself immediately upon them and killed them by drinking their blood to the last drop.

'According to the legend the life of the monster was lengthened by the number of years which each of his victims would havc lived if he had not killed them, so that he would have lived forever if someone had not discovered that the only means of exterminating him consisted in lodging a silver ball [ie bullet] in his head.'

This 'legend' is a shameless work of fiction. The only other writer to make claims for vampires in Wales is Marie Trevelyan, in her *Folk-Lore and Folk-Stories of Wales*, published in 1909. It is hard to say how reliable Trevelyan is as a collector of folklore, but she does tell some interesting stories.

For example, in relation to a 'reputed witch' of the Vale of Neath, she wrote:

'After her death the few friends she had shut up the room and sat by the fire all night. During their vigil they repeatedly heard a scratching noise in the death-chamber, but were afraid to enter it. In the morning they found the witch's body covered with innumerable marks as if by suction. Then the women said vampires had been at work all night, and the funeral was hastened, "for fear the body would be entirely devoured".'

Trevelyan's book can lay claim to perhaps the strangest vampires on record: *vampire furniture*.

One of these was a chair in an old Glamorganshire house which would 'bite' the hands of any clergyman who sat in it, drawing blood. More horrible was the vampire bed in a house in Cardiff. This apparently sucked the life out of a poor little baby. On the body of the dead child was a red mark and the doctor who examined it said: 'It was just as though something had caught at the child's throat and sucked the blood, as one would suck an egg.'

The grieving father later slept in the bed and also felt his life ebbing away. He survived but found a similar red mark on his throat. Amazingly, the family did not throw away the bed (or burn it) but kept it in a spare room. Trevelyan claimed to have seen it there.

Old Welsh country furniture is making high prices on the antiques market right now. This well cared for old bed may even now be on display in some emporium, just waiting for an unwitting purchaser . . .

Sources: The 1890 volume of *Bye-gones; Folk-Lore and Folk-Stories of Wales* by Marie Trevelyan.

Witchcraft and magic

The oldest fear

Arguably the oldest superstition known to mankind is that a person can use supernatural forces to do another harm – that is to say, the belief in witchcraft.

Wales, in common with the rest of the world, has a rich folklore regarding witches. Elias Owen gives a list of attributes of Welsh witches in his *Welsh Folklore*:

'They were able to travel in the air on a broom-stick; make children ill; give maids the nightmare; curse with madness, animals; bring misfortune on families; hinder the dairy maid from making butter; and many more imaginary things were placed to their credit.'

Usually witches were identified with solitary, reputedly bad-tempered old women living in hovels with nothing for company but a pet, thought of as a 'familiar devil', but there was also a widespread belief in midnight meetings of witches on bare mountains and in old ruins, where they would plot the downfall of their neighbours and pay allegiance to their master, the devil. Moel y Parc in the Clwydian Range, now home to a prominent transmitter mast, was said to be one of their meeting places.

It appears that at one time every parish had its supposed witch. Among the most notorious, however, was an entire family, known as the Llanddona Witches. The whole crew turned up one morning near the village of Llanddona on the north coast of Anglesey. They had been cast adrift in a boat without oars, from where no one knew. At first the suspicious villagers tried to repel them, but when they magically brought forth a useful spring out of the earth, the villagers allowed them to stay. This proved to be a mistake.

The men were fierce fighters who made their living by smuggling. The women were blackmailers, preying on their superstitious neighbours. As Owen explains:

'The women, with dishevelled hair, and bared breasts, visited farm houses and requested charity, more as a right than a favour, and no one dared refuse them. Taking advantage of the credulity of the people, they cursed those whom they disliked.'

Perhaps the belief in witchcraft persisted as long as it did because so many anti-social people found they could frighten food and favours out of people by pretending to be witches. Unfortunately, they often paid the price of their con act by being attacked or even killed – often by the official judiciary.

Source: *Welsh Folklore* by Elias Owen.

Rough justice

The witch-burning hysteria which led to the deaths of many innocent women and not a few men in Europe and parts of England never infected Wales, and witch trials of any sort were comparatively rare. Nevertheless, belief in witchcraft seemed to linger longer here and there are some surprising – and shocking – accounts of supposed witches being assaulted in Wales well into the nineteenth century.

One of the many annoyances Welsh witches were supposed to inflict upon their neighbours was preventing the churning of butter. Milk refusing to churn was a common frustration on farms in the past and it was as easy to blame it on witchcraft as it is for us today to blame the unreliability of our cars on gremlins.

Trivial though it seems, one unfortunate woman found herself accused of being a witch, and was assaulted as a result, just because a neighbour's butter wouldn't churn. This happened as late as 1830, at Llanfyllin, in Powys.

On March 25th of that year, the young farmer who had bullied her was brought before the local magistrates. His victim explained: 'The defendant came to my house, and prevailed upon me against my will to accompany him home, and then made me kneel down before the churn and repeat these words: "The blessing of God be on the milk."

'On remonstrating with him he pierced a nail through my hand until the blood flowed.'

The poor old woman showed her wounded hand to the magistrates. When asked what he thought he was about, the unrepentant farmer replied that he had often had difficulty churning butter and 'thought it best to get the woman to bless the milk'.

The magistrates were told it was 'a common belief among the old people that to draw the blood out of a witch would prevent her witching anyone else'. The farmer was not only found guilty of assault, but was also told off for believing in witchcraft in the first place.

This case is not an isolated one. A few years earlier an even more shocking assault on a supposed witch took place in Monmouthshire. A farmer, a constable and two farm servants accosted a woman in her nineties, believing her to have bewitched some cattle. First they forced her on her knees and made her repeat a prayer intended to remove a curse from the cattle. Then they too drew blood:

'the prisoners, under the stupid notion that if you draw a witch's blood she cannot hurt you, took a bough of wild rose out of a hedge and drew this across her arm, so as to make it bleed.'

Further indignities followed. The elderly woman was stripped to the waist in front of a growing crowd of onlookers and then had her hair cut off. One of the men then suggested ducking their victim. Ducking was an old method to try a witch – the accused was thrown into a body of water and if she floated it proved she had supernatural powers. If she sank, however, she was innocent . . . and had probably drowned.

Entreaties by the old woman's daughter dissuaded them from this extreme act, which was just as well, as was pointed out by the magistrates before whom these men were later brought – they might otherwise have ended up being charged with her murder.

Before sentencing, the chairman of the magistrates told the court that 'the prisoners had acted under a delusion founded on superstition . . . and he regretted that there was anyone in the kingdom who should have been so deploringly ignorant as to have fallen into such an error.'

Sources: The 1882 and 1894 volumes of *Bye-gones*.

Curses!

It is hard to imagine today, but the charming village of Llanelian-yn-Rhos, in Conwy, was once the centre of a kind of Welsh voodoo cult.

Near the village, which is situated a few miles south of Colwyn Bay, there was a well called Ffynnon Elian, which was named after the local saint. For some reason that is now obscure, this former holy well became a cursing well.

The folklorist Marie Trevelyan recorded the sinister ritual that was employed there, using the example of a farmer's wife who wished to revenge herself on her husband, whom she suspected of infidelity:

'She made a figure of marl [a kind of clay] and stuck it with pins in the place where the heart should be. She then registered [her husband's] name in the clerk's book and lowered the marl figure into the water. There it remained for a week, during which her husband suffered tortures of pain in his heart.'

The 'clerk' would charge a hefty sum for the use of the well, but he would also contact those who were due to be cursed, and offer to remove their names for another big fee. All in all, it was a highly lucrative scam, which, by the eighteenth century, was doing a roaring trade.

Having become a scandal to the district, the operation at the well was finally shut down in 1828 and the conmen imprisoned. The well was finally filled-in in the late 19th century, and no sign of its whereabouts now remain.

Another folklorist, the Rev. Elias Owen, was officiating at a funeral for a farmer's wife in Trefeglwys, Powys, and was surprised to notice that the farm owner, who had been prominent in the procession to church, was not present at the ceremony. Later he asked why this should be – and was amazed by the reply.

He was informed that the gentleman 'had been put into Ffynnon Elian because of some love affair, that he had found himself ailing after he had been cursed, and that he himself had gone to the well to ascertain whether the fair revenger had been there before him; this, he found, had been the case'.

Greatly alarmed, the man had asked whether there was a way he might avoid the curse? The guardian of the well said that – for a consideration, of course – he might be able to help. In the event, the cursed man was told he would be free of the evil effects if he kept within the confines of his own estate and never again left its borders.

'With these hard terms he complied,' explains the Rev. Owen, 'and from early manhood to old age, he had never been known to go beyond the limits of his small estate. He lived this exile for the length of an ordinary man's life. He was social enough when visited, and he would occasionally accompany any stray caller upon him to the boundary of his property, and then return to his voluntary prison.'

On the day of the funeral, he had accompanied the cortege as far as the conditions of the curse allowed him, and then had gone quietly home.

Sources: *Folk-Lore and Folk-Stories of Wales* by Marie Trevelyan and the 1882 volume of *Bye-gones*. See plate 3.

Charmed, I'm not so sure

About the year 1845 a deacon of a church in Machynlleth was brought before his elders – accused of practising witchcraft. Hotly he denied the charge, but then he hung his head in shame. He had to own up that it was partly true.

He explained that the country people thereabouts had got it into their heads that he was some sort of 'cunning man', that he could conjure and command spirits, and that it was in his power to ward off bad luck or the evil attentions of witches. He insisted that he had repeatedly assured his neighbours that none of this was true, but in the end he had sought to satisfy them by writing out 'charms' – passages in Latin which they could hide around their homes and farms to magically protect them.

Of course, it did not take long for the supposedly harassed deacon to start charging for his services . . .

Not surprisingly, the young man was dragged over the coals for such un-Christian behaviour, but as the investigation continued, the facts became more shocking. It transpired that one of the elders of the church had himself made use of the deacon's 'powers'. This good old Christian firmly believed his cow had been bewitched and the deacon wrote out a protective charm which the older man then fed to the animal.

It's hard to believe this was taking place in Victorian times, at the height of scientific and technological progress. But old beliefs die hard. The 'man of knowledge' – *y dyn hysbys* in Welsh – was an important figure in rural Wales. They were often men with a little learning who had fallen on hard times through bad luck or, often, because of drink.

Scanty though their learning might be, it was quite enough to fool and frighten their totally uneducated and gullible neighbours.

Many of these sorcerers became well-known. The wonderfully named Dic Spot the Conjuror, who lived in Oswestry in the eighteenth century, was rich enough to have servants and a carriage. By the end of his life he insisted on being paid in gold for his services, which usually involved the discovery of thefts or the removal of troublesome ghosts.

Occasionally, charms such as those written out by the Machynlleth deacon are found in old Welsh homes. One was found behind the plaster in a cottage near Chirk, Wrexham. Surrounded by strange hieroglyphics and cabbalistic symbols was this fiery passage:

'In the Name of God let god arise and scatter these mine Enemies let Them Be as The Dust before The Wind and The Angel of The Lord scattering Them . . . Put on the whole Armour of God That we may be able to stand against the Devil . . . Dei gratia illum quod Sacrument Ingrato . . . '

Sources:The 1892 volume of *Bye-gones;A Charm from Chirk* by Trefor M Owen in the *Denbighshire Historical Society Transactions*.

The Pig o' the Brook

One of the least salubrious yet most celebrated of the conjurers who eked out a living by foxing their uneducated and superstitious neighbours with their own scanty knowledge was the ill-named Mochyn-y-Nant, or 'The Pig o' the Brook'.

Mochyn-y-Nant lived in the village of Pen-y-cae, near Wrexham, two hundred years ago. He appears to have earned his name from the poor state of his hygiene, but this didn't prevent him earning a reputation as a sorcerer of great power. Indeed, after his death, a pamphlet was published extolling his successes:

'By Magic Spells the Pig o' the Brook
The Village Pilferer oft took;
The Fortune of each Girl he knew,
And if her Swain were false or true;
He'd rule the Planets, too, they say,
And tell both Birth and Bridal Day ...
Could Dreams expound or Lay a Ghost
In the Red Sea with Pharoah's Host:
Each Thought before him stood confess'd,
Which made Folks think he was possess'd.'

And so on and so forth.

A fascinating meeting with Mochyn-y-Nant was recorded by Thomas de Quincey – the self-styled Opium Eater – who visited the sorcerer in 1802 while staying with friends in the Wrexham area. He writes:

'There was a folornness and an ancient tarnish ... which

went far to justify the name [of 'Pig']. Speaking humanely, one would have insinuated that the stargazer wanted much washing and scouring; but, astrologically speaking, perhaps he would have been spoiled by earthly water for the celestial vigils.'

Having asked pertinent questions about de Quincey's birth time, the Pig o' the Brook then retired alone to a backroom with a folio book – which he claimed was an original hand-written treatise – and a large bottle of port. He returned half an hour later 'even more lugubrious' than before, and in a dreadful voice prophesised doom for the hugely entertained de Quincey.

The author willingly paid up the fee of a few pieces of silver and managed to take a peek at Mochyn-y-Nant's treasured book of magic, which he saw was in fact a perfectly ordinary printed book with its covers missing.

Charlatan though he no doubt was, the Pig o' the Brook's personality was sufficiently larger than life to have earned himself a place in folklore forever.

Source: The 1874 volume of *Bye-gones; The Black Arts in Wrexham* by D Leslie Davies, in the *Denbighshire Historical Society Transactions*.

Weather retort

One of Flintshire's most impressive ancient monuments is Maen Chwyfan, a stone preaching cross nearly four metres high which was erected in the tenth or eleventh centuries in the corner of a field near Whitford.

The cross probably marks the site where Chwyfan, an early Welsh saint, preached to the populace. It is wonderfully ornamented, with strange animals and little spear-bearing warriors hiding among a foliage of knotwork which runs up the shaft to the discoid cross. It is known as a 'wheel cross', and it is the tallest of its kind in Britain.

Despite its age, the monument is in a remarkable state of preservation. This may be due to the fact that it was able to defend itself – anyone interfering with Maen Chwyfan would get zapped by lightning.

According to an account published in 1879, country people fancied it covered some treasure, and now and again tried to undermine it. However, they were always thwarted in their designs 'by a sudden storm of thunder and lightning'.

In 1900, the same thing is reported: 'Three or four successive attempts were made by some monks to see what the stone covered and on each occasion the attempt had to be given up by reason of the lightning. The singular part of the matter is that days were chosen when lightning would be least, but to no avail.'

Who these monks were or what they were after is not recorded. The irony is that Maen Chwyfan was thoroughly excavated in the eighteenth century and nothing was found.

The druids were said to have magical power over the elements, including the ability to raise storms, and the early Celtic saints, such as St Chwyfan, are described as being similarly magical. Legends describe sudden storms springing up to defend supposed sites of valuable hoards all over Wales.

For example, a great treasure was believed to have been buried on the hill fort of Moel Arthur in the Clwydian Range. Tantalisingly, a mysterious light would always shine at night to reveal the precise location of the hoard, tempting many to seek it out. However, once they had found the treasure chest, even to the point of grasping its iron handle, a terrible squall of wind would blow up, so severe that the treasure seekers would be driven back, their booty unclaimed.

When a party of Victorian antiquarians, intent on more legitimate excavations, were forced to abandon their work by drenching wet weather, they were met by an old woman who lived in a cottage near the bottom of Moel Arthur, and she told them: 'Whoever digs there is always driven away by thunder and lightning and storm; you have been served like everyone else who made the attempt.'

I too have experienced something similar. I was in the company of Scott Lloyd (co-author of *The Lost Legend of Arthur* and *The Keys to Avalon*), exploring a summit on the Denbigh moors, when we found what our imaginations suggested was an ancient burial place. We were just trudging up to investigate when were assaulted by a sudden and totally unexpected onslaught of stinging hail, driven so hard by the wind that it was coming at us horizontally. We very soon gave up our investigation and headed back down towards the car. As soon as we were a hundred yards from the 'burial', the hail stopped, the wind died and the sun came out again.

Of course, the cynical may make reference to the unpredictability of the Welsh weather . . . the fact that we were on a mountain top and so on. And those who are also of an antiquarian frame of mind will chide us for our feebleness. All I can say in answer to such critics is – they weren't there!

Sources: The ancient monuments report for Flintshire; the 1912 volume of *Cheshire Sheaf; Folk-Lore and Folk Stories of Wales* by Marie Trevelyan; the 1850 volume of *Archaeologia Cambrensis*; the 1877 volume of *Bye-gones*. See plate 30

Making an impression

Certain people can hold such sway on the imagination that they quite literally leave their mark.

Take Wales' most popular hero, Owain Glyndŵr, for example. Legend has it that he once threw a dagger with such force that it left behind a dagger-shaped mark on the stone it struck. This miracle can still be seen today, but in a rather unglamorous position – lain over an unused door above a septic tank at Corwen church.

The fifteenth century prince also left his footprint embedded in a rock above Corwen and his knee-prints on another rock just outside the town. The 'footprint' is especially convincing.

A recent book draws my attention to these curios: *Footprints in Stone* by Janet Bord (Heart of Albion press, 2004). Janet, who lives in Denbighshire, has several books to her name, including *Fairies: Real Encounters with Little People*, and many more written with her husband Colin *(Mysterious Britain, Modern Mysteries of the World* and *Alien Animals*, for example). In *Footprints in Stone*, Janet claims that it is a common trait for larger-than-life or especially holy people to be commemorated in this way – that various impressions or shapes in the landscape become connected to them. In this way even real, historical figures like Owain Glyndŵr are made superhuman.

There are examples from all over the world, but Wales has more than its share. Janet Bord also discusses the existence of a supposed footprint of the Virgin Mary at Llanfair, between Barmouth and Harlech. According to legend, Mary visited Wales, and she embarked from her ship at this stretch of coastline. Not only did the Virgin leave her footprint in the stone at Llanfair, but also her thumbprint, and the imprints of her knees and her breast when she knelt to pray. A rock on Bardsey Island bears her handprint.

Not just people but also the animals they rode could create footprints – or hoofprints, rather. King Arthur's horse left hoofprints at Loggerheads, near Mold, and Llyn Barfog, near Aberdyfi. St George's horse left behind hoofprints at the village of St George in Denbighshire, where, as local legend informs us, the fight with the dragon took place.

My favourite story concerns two depressions in a rock near Llanymawddwy. Apparently, these were caused by the Dark Age king Maelgwn Gwynedd. He rested here after hunting, but the stone just happened to be the favourite seat of a local saint. As a result, Maelgwn's bum became magically stuck to it. The petulant saint eventually released the king from this undignified position – but the marks of his buttocks are still there to be seen.

Sources: *Old Stone Crosses of the Vale of Clwyd* by Elias Owen; *Footprints in Stone* by Janet Bord. See plate 29.

Mysterious monuments

Mysterious Island

Jules Verne may not have had Anglesey in mind when he wrote *Mysterious Island*, but it seems a fair name for the place. Ynys Môn is full of mystery. A former stronghold of the Druids, there are more ancient monuments there per square mile than anywhere else in Wales. Prehistoric tombs, mounds and standing stones litter the landscape, and many have strange stories attached to them.

The Carreg Leidr *(a thief stone)* stands in a field near Maenaddwyn, west of Brynteg. According to legend, a thief was running away with his booty when he was magically transformed into a stone for his wickedness. At certain angles, the Carreg Leidr monolith does rather look like a man with a bag of swag on his shoulder.

Nearer Brynteg there is a boulder called the Cadair-y-Bwgan, or 'Chair of the Goblin'. The goblin was 'a terrifying phantom' who would torment the local farmers by throwing things about and 'befouling the dairies'. When it became bored with causing mayhem, the *bwgan* (or goblin) would sit in this 'chair' by the roadside and frighten passers-by instead. This plain lump of rock is not classed as an ancient monument, but the fact that it has such a strange story attached to it suggests that it did have some significance in the distant past.

The most striking story attached to a prehistoric monument in Anglesey is that told about the Lligwy Cromlech, a burial chamber near Moelfre.

Many, many years ago, the story goes, a fisherman on his way down to the sea saw somebody struggling in the storm-lashed waves. Without a thought for his own safety, he dived in and helped the struggling swimmer to shore. He found he had rescued a beautiful woman wearing a robe of white and jewelled bracelets. She begged the fisherman to help her up the hill to 'the huge stone', by which she meant the cromlech, a burial chamber that has an enormous low-lying boulder as its roof.

The fisherman waited patiently while the woman regained her breath, keen to ask her how she had found herself in such peril. But she anticipated his question, and, speaking in a harsh, croaking voice, quite out of keeping with her charming appearance, she astonished him with the words: 'I am a witch, and was thrown off a ship in Lligwy Bay. If I had been swimming in my usual raiment you would have allowed me to sink – but I disguised myself.'

The fisherman shrank back in terror, but the witch was grateful to him. She gave him a small sphere containing a charm of snake skin and told him that so long as he kept it safe, he and his family would enjoy endless good luck.

The fisherman buried the charm near the cromlech. An hour later he saw the witch leaping from rock to rock in Lligwy Bay in order to reach a ship that was waiting for her – and that was the last he saw of her.

The charm remained safe for many years, and the fisherman's family enjoyed remarkable runs of luck, prospering more and more every year. One day it vanished, however, and the good luck ceased. But some time later a dying neighbour confessed to stealing it and he returned it to its rightful owner.

Good luck was with the family again, and the charm followed members to Australia and then to India, where it was last heard of in the 1860s.

I wonder where the mysterious sphere is now, and whether it is still bringing good fortune to its possessor.

Sources: The 1914 volume of the *Anglesey Antiquarian Society Transactions* and *Folk-Lore and Folk-Stories of Wales* by Marie Trevelyan. I am also indebted to Michael Bayley Hughes and Gwyn Llewelyn for letting me know of the Cadair-y-Bwgan's whereabouts. See plate 6.

Stones of power

Recently I went looking for a prehistoric standing stone that was recorded in 1929 but which was not marked on the modern Ordnance Survey map. To my surprise, I found it, but what really surprised me was just how easy it was to find – it stands right by the side of the road and is over five foot tall.

The Pant-y-Maen standing stone is near Bryneglwys in Denbighshire. Its disappearance from our maps is mysterious but the stone is unusual for another reason too: it is standing on top of a burial mound. This is very rare – it is the sort of feature you might see in an illustration for a Tolkien story, but not out in the field. (The burial mound, incidentally, *is* marked on the map, as 'Tumulus'.)

The main reason I wanted to find this stone was the interesting story attached to it. The stone and its mound were described in 1929 in *The Prehistoric and Roman Remains of Denbighshire* by an amateur archaeologist named Ellis Davies. Davies reported that in the 1860s a man named Edward Roberts, of the nearby farm of Penybedw, decided that the monument would prove useful as a gate-post. He had it dragged away for that purpose. He suffered so much disorder of mind and lack of sleep after removing it, however, that he had it returned to its original position, and a neighbour, Enoch Morris, ensured that no one else would tamper with the stone by planting a yew tree on either side of it with a hedgerow in between.

The yew trees are still there, as are the remains of the hawthorn hedge.

The standing stone can be found at GR 158477

(Ordnance Survey Explorer 256), on top of the tumulus and opposite a gate marked Pant-y-Maen (Hollow of the Stone), the name of a nearby cottage. There is a lay-by right by the stone.

There is a similar, but even more bizarre tale told about a standing stone in Anglesey.

On the south coast of the island, below Brynsiencyn, the hamlet of Llanidan basks peacefully in rural isolation. A fine manor house, a couple of farm-houses, a few cottages and a church make up a scene which is as timeless as it is charming. The church was once much larger than it is today and is now partly in ruins. It has a distinctly spooky, Hammer House of Horror look.

Cemented into the inside wall of the church there was once a mysterious stone, which vaguely resembled a human leg, a shape that earn it the name of Maen Morddwyd *(the thigh stone)*. The resemblance to a leg didn't end with its appearance, however – reputedly it could also walk!

If the Maen Morddwyd was ever taken away from Llanidan, it would make its own way back. On hearing of the stone's perambulatory prowess, the arrogant Earl Hugh of Chester decided to put it to the test. He chained it to a bigger rock and dumped it in the Menai Strait. Despite his efforts, Maen Morddwyd was found back in its usual position inside the church the next morning. Cementing it into the wall put a stop to its rambles, however.

The stone is long gone but the church is said to contain another miracle: a holy water stoup which is never found empty, although it is never filled.

Sources: *Prehistoric and Roman Remains in Denbighshire* by Ellis

Davies; *More Mysterious Wales* by Chris Barber. The story of Maen Morddwyd was originally recorded in the Middle Ages. See plates 4 and 5.

Two neglected monuments

Situated in a lonely field in Anglesey is one of the oldest and largest ancient monuments in Wales, and also one of the least well-known.

This is the Henblas Dolmen, a grouping of three colossal boulders which once sheltered a prehistoric burial. It is unknown whether these massive rocks – each much taller than a man – are a natural feature or whether they were somehow moved there deliberately. Some think they were left behind by the movement of glaciers during the Ice Age.

They are very roughly shaped, with no indication of workmanship upon them. Nevertheless, it seems an extraordinary coincidence that three rocks each composed almost exclusively of quartz should have been deposited here together, in an area otherwise devoid of such stones. Quartz is a mineral that is often given pride of place in ancient sacred sites, and the rocks which make up the Henblas Dolmen shimmer with crystal, some of it white, some of it pink.

Whatever its origin, the presence of a burial (the word 'dolmen' implies a burial place) suggests that the site was once considered sacred. An urn containing burnt bones and a ring of blue glass was found in the space enclosed by the rocks.

There is a tradition that an avenue of stones formerly led up to the Henblas Dolmen from the river below. If so, the sight of the brilliant white boulders shining in the sun at the top of the hill must have made an impressive sight to anyone approaching that way.

Henblas itself is a small country park based around a show

farm a few miles south-east of Llangefni; it is clearly signposted from the A5. Permission must be sought to visit the Dolmen.

Better known but even more woefully neglected considering its size and extraordinary state of preservation is Tre'r Ceiri – *the home of the giants*. Tre'r Ceiri is a stone-walled fortress built by the Celts about AD70, the time of the Roman invasion.

It is perched on the southernmost peak of Yr Eifl in northern Llŷn. Despite being nearly two thousand years old, the original stone enclosure still survives, as do the ruins of the 'round-huts' in which the people lived. Round-huts usually only survive as circular marks on the ground, of interest to the most imaginative archaeologists, so the preserved structures are extraordinary. But it is the virtually intact wall, six feet high in places, which really takes the breath away. There is even a kind of bridge, intact in the centre of the wall. It is strange to think it was built in about the same year that Jerusalem was falling to the Romans.

No wonder the place was treated with some suspicion by our more recent forefathers. Many prehistoric structures became associated with giants in our folklore, so it is no surprise that this dramatic fortress earned the name of being a home for giants.

However, it is a story recorded in 1856 that really sets it apart. This tells of a warrior named Cilmyn, who had a friend who was a 'necromancer' (i.e. a wizard who converses with spirits). The necromancer told the knight that Tre'r Ceiri was the lair of a demon and his wife, and that in their possession was a magical book, which had been written 'by no human hand'.

Cilmyn agreed to get the book for the wizard, and the

story tells of how he fought all the demons inhabiting the stone huts to acquire it. The story is rather *Lord of the Rings*, but as the sea mist sweeps over the mountain and you pick your way back through the ancient habitations, your surroundings all but obscured, you may find yourself able to believe it.

Sources: *The Modern Antiquarian* by Julian Cope; the ancient monuments report for Caernarfonshire; the 1856 volume of the *Cambrian Register*. See plates 27 and 28.

The Welsh pyramids

Rising like an earthen pyramid above the north Flintshire village of Trelawnyd, The Gop is one of Britain's most interesting yet least understood archaeological sites.

Its purpose and origins are a mystery – a big mystery. The Gop is the second largest prehistoric mound in Europe, the largest being Silbury Hill in Wiltshire. The Gop is an awe-inspiring forty-five foot high and between two hundred and three hundred feet round.

Why was such a huge mound elevated there? One theory is that The Gop was used as the base of a beacon, an idea that is suggested by the far-reaching views it commands (it has been said 'Gop' is a corruption of 'gawp', because this is what people do when they reach the summit).

Another popular idea is that it is a huge burial mound. According to local tradition – entirely unsupported by archeological evidence – The Gop was the last resting place of the famous warrior queen Boudica, who waged war on the Romans and who was known to them as Boadicea and to the Welsh as Buddug.

In fact, like its big brother Silbury Hill, The Gop contains no burials at all – it's just a big pile of earth and rock. However, in a cave situated thirty feet below the mound, and a hundred feet to the south-west of it, fourteen skeletons, together with other human remains, were found. The bodies had been interred there over successive generations, suggesting that this was a very sacred spot in the Bronze Age. It is possible the mound was erected to mark the presence of this sacred cave.

Its obscure origin is one of the mysteries pertaining to

The Gop, but the other is why it is so little known.

The Gop can be accessed from the village of Trelawnyd, off the A5151 coast road. Use an Ordnance Survey map or ask a friendly resident to direct you to either of the two footpaths up to the site.

Another 'Welsh pyramid' can be found on the west coast of Anglesey, near Aberffraw. Barclodiad y Gawres is one of the most impressive burial mounds in Britain. It dates from the Stone Age. A twenty foot passage leads to a central chamber, where burials were found, along with a mysterious burnt offering, which was described by the archaeologists who excavated the site in 1953 as a 'witch's brew' – it contained the remains of pig, fish, frog, toad, snake, mouse, shrew and hare.

Five of the stones leading to the chamber are ornamented with spiral and zigzag designs, suggesting the chamber had a ritual as well as a burial function. Many people believe that these mounds represent the pregnancy of a pre-Christian goddess, and there is certainly something womb-like about the entrance ways and dark interiors of such places.

The name of this mound is interesting. *Gawres* is welsh for Giantess and a *barclod* was a kind of apron worn by Welsh country women. The name roughly translates as 'The Giantess's Apronful'. This strange name is explained by a legend that a Giantess was carrying a huge stone in her apron to be used in a sacred altar and she dropped it here. The same name is shared by a tumulus near Bwlch y Ddeufan in Gwynedd and also by a natural outcrop of rock at Llanrhaeadr in Powys.

The huge hound of Barclodiad y Gawres, perched on a headland overlooking the sea, is impressive, but to gain access to its interior, you will need a key, for it is always kept padlocked. The key is available on payment of a deposit from the Wayside Stores at nearby Llanfaelog. It is well worth a trip, as is the smaller but equally fascinating Bryn Celli Ddu burial chamber in the south of the island at Llanddaniel Fab.

Sources: *Prehistoric and Roman Remains in Flintshire* by Ellis Davies; and the ancient monuments report for Anglesey. See plates 9 and 10.

A mountain of legend

Wales is a land of legends but there is one place which is more abundant in stories than any other. This is a fortified hill in Denbighshire: Dinas Brân. With its distinctive conical shape surmounted by the ruins of a medieval castle, Dinas Brân is a dramatic feature of the Vale of Llangollen. It is a very ancient place. Before the castle was built, there was a prehistoric hill fort here.

Dinas Brân features in the legends of King Arthur and the quest for the Holy Grail. The Grail was variously described as a cup used at the Last Supper, or a vessel which collected Christ's blood during the Passion. Arthur and his Knights of the Round Table set off in quest of the Grail as a symbol of all that is pure and holy.

In one medieval Romance, the castle in which the Grail is kept is clearly identified as Dinas Brân, under the Norman French name of 'Chastiel Bron'. Bron was given as the name of the keeper of the Grail.

In fact 'Brân' translates as raven and was the name of a legendary king of Wales, Brân the Blessed. In the medieval Welsh tales, the Maginogi, Brân was an enormous giant, who waded across the Irish Sea to rescue his sister, Branwen, from the King of Ireland. Although he rescued Branwen, he was fatally wounded in the attempt. He urged his followers to cut off his head and return with it to Ynys Prydain (the Isle of Britain). Having accomplished this gruesome deed, they sailed away, first to Anglesey (where poor Branwen, who died of a broken heart, was buried) and then around the British Isles for about eighty years, magically sustained by the head of Brân, which could not only chat away merrily but was also able to conjure up food from nowhere and slow down time so that his followers hardly aged a day.

Eventually the giant's head was buried under 'the White Hill', positioned so that it faced out to sea. Brân said that as long as his head remained buried there, no one would be able to invade Ynys Prydain. One story says that the White Hill is where the Tower of London now stands, and the famous ravens in the Tower are there in remembrance of Brân – it is said that if the ravens should ever fly away, Britain will fall. The latter tradition appears to have been a Victorian embellishment, but an older tale also returns to the head of Brân – mighty King Arthur is supposed to have dug it up to show that no one except himself was needed to keep Ynys Prydain safe. Alas, as soon as he had disturbed the head of Brân, the Saxons invaded.

Brân was not the only giant to inhabit Dinas Brân. Shortly after the Norman conquest, the castle was haunted by a hideous ogre called Goemagog, who was killed, after a bloody battle, by one of the knights of King William the First.

Rather more likeable is the lovelorn minstrel who features in another story associated with Dinas Brân. He fell in love with a maiden, who spurned his advances despite his exquisite musicianship. In despair, he played a beautiful elegy in her honour and in front of everyone in the banqueting hall . . . he faded away to nothingness.

There is also a legend of goblins haunting the slopes of Dinas Brân and a tradition that a fabulous treasure (perhaps the Holy Grail) lies buried somewhere on its summit. The treasure will one day be discovered by a fair-haired boy who owns a silver dog which can see the wind. One account describes the treasure as a golden raven – which takes the story back to Brân the Blessed again.

Sources: *Brân the Blessed in Arthurian Romance* by Helaine Newstead; *A Pedestrian Tour of Northern Wales* by G.J. Bennett; *The Welsh Fairy Book* by W. Jenkins Thomas. See plate 11.

Great evil overcome

The Clwydian Range of hills which divide Denbighshire from Flintshire is rich in history and romance. As well as links to King Arthur, there is a very old tale about a giant, but one quite different from Brân the Blessed.

Moel Fenlli, the hill directly south of the Clwydians' highest peak, Moel Fama, is crowned by an ancient hill fort with very well preserved defensive banks and ditches. Moel Fenlli is believed to have been named after Benlli, a Dark Age prince.

Benlli is usually referred to as Benlli Gawr, the latter word probably best translating in this context as 'Great', in the same kind of construction as 'Alexander the Great' or 'Peter the Great'. 'Gawr' also means 'giant' and the story deserides Benlli as an imposing giant of a man and a cruel tyrant.

In the legend, a local missionary, St Garmon, called on Benlli Gawr with the intention of converting him and his wild band of warriors to Christianity. Benlli snubbed the holy man, however, and sent his lowliest servant, a swineherd named Cadell, to send him about his business.

Cadell was the only decent fellow in Benlli's court. He secretly took St Garmon to his humble cottage and in his honour slaughtered one of his two cows to provide him with dinner. This was a great sacrifice for such a poor man, and St Garmon was grateful for it. He prayed to God and the slaughtered calf was found alive and whole again the next morning.

This was not the only result of St Garmon's prayer, however. Benlli's court was destroyed by a blazing fire from the sky, making it a kind of Welsh Sodom or Gomorrah. Cadell the swineherd – now converted to Christianity – was made King of Powys as a small thank you for his kindness to God's emissary, St Garmon.

Another legend has it that Benlli and St Garmon also had an encounter in Mold, although whether this preceded or post-dated the destruction of Benlli's court is not clear. Garmon had founded a small community of Christians at Mold, and Benlli, with a band of mercenary Picts, came to destroy it. The Christians – anything but fighting men – were guided by St Garmon to ambush Benlli's force as they entered a hollow near the town. On his command, the Christians all leapt to their feet, crying 'Alleluia! Alleluia!' The effect was so dramatic that the Picts, fearing they had been surprised by a much larger and fearsome band of men than was the case, immediately fled.

The rabble was routed and Garmon's community continued to live in peace. The site of the adventure still bears the name Maes Garmon (Garmon's Place) and an obelisk commemorates the legendary skirmish.

Source: The tale of Benlli Gawr first appeared in ninth century *Historia Brittonum*, attributed to the Scribe Nennius. See plate 12.

The home of Arthur

Up against the wall of venerable Exmewe House, now Barclay's Bank, in St Peter's Square, Ruthin, can be found a rough-hewn boulder of limestone.

This is Maen Huail *(the stone of Huail)*. Huail, after whom it is named, has been claimed as the brother of Gildas the Monk, one of Britain's earliest historians. A local legend claims that Huail was a mighty warrior, rival in power to none other than King Arthur himself.

The legend of Maen Huail appeared in a chronicle written in about the year 1530 by one Elis Gruffudd, who lived in the Flintshire parish of Ysceifiog. Arthur, states this legend, discovered Huail consorting with one of his mistresses. The ensuing row soon turned into a fight. Huail, however, was the victor, and wounded Arthur in the knee. Arthur agreed that this should be the end of the quarrel, but he put Huail under a strict ban never to refer to the wound he had inflicted. Then he limped off to his court at Caerwys.

Sometime later, Arthur was in Ruthin, cavorting with another girl. For some reason, not properly explained, the warrior had disguised himself in female clothing to accomplish this, but the disguise did not fool Huail, who also happened to be present. He saw Arthur dancing and laughed out: 'The dancing would be fine if it wasn't for your knee!' In so doing, he had broken his formal promise to Arthur never to mention the wound.

Arthur was furious and it wasn't long before Huail found himself placed in custody. Arthur had him dragged over to a nearby boulder and there, with his own sword, he beheaded

Huail, so ending a feud that had undermined his power for years.

Ever since, the stone has been known as Maen Huail, and it remains one of the most important surviving relics associated with the Arthurian legend.

Overlooking Ruthin is the Clwydian Range of hills, which is not only beautiful but also of great historical interest. Here there are more hill forts than in any other comparable area in the British Isles. One of the most prominent of these is Moel Arthur – a name which can hardly fail to be suggestive.

Was this fortress used by the legendary King Arthur? Possibly – and for two reasons. Firstly, an ancient Welsh poem refers to a warrior fighting 'like Arthur at Caer Fenlli', and Foel Fenlli is another fortified hill in the Clwydian Range. The second reason is more complicated. According to legend, when Arthur is severely wounded, he is taken to a mystical place called Avalon. Avalon should really be spelled the old Welsh way: Afallon. Now, Afallon was the home of a man named Afallwch, and although there is nowhere (of any age) named 'Afallon', one place in Britain can be found which is named after Afallwch. This is another prehistoric hill fort, Caerfallwch, whose name translates as 'Fortress of Afallwch'. This may perhaps be Afallon . . .

Caerfallwch is perched above the Flintshire village of Rhosesmor and is situated directly east of Moel Arthur. If you stand, as I did, in the entrance to the hill fort on Moel Arthur you will see Caerfallwch neatly framed. On the old Celtic spirit night of Beltane – the 31st of April – I was once on Moel Arthur waiting to see the May Day sunrise. I stood in the ramparts facing east, and was most impressed to see the sun rise directly above Caerfallwch, framed by the entranceway of the ancient fortress.

Arthur – Afallon and Afallon – Arthur. Intriguing . . .

Source: For more on Arthur's connections to Wales, seek out The Lost Legend of Arthur by Steve Blake and Scott Lloyd, published in 2002 by Rider. See plate 13.

Old customs
and other survivals

Sacred waters

The shrine of St Winefride's is one of the most exquisite medieval buildings in Wales. It covers a holy well which has been a place of pilgrimage since the early days of the Celtic church. So famous was it that the town in which it is situated was named after it – Holywell, in Flintshire.

The legend behind the well is that it sprang out of the ground where a holy virgin, Winefride, was martyred. A hot-headed local youth cut off her head when she resisted his advances. Fortunately, Winefride's uncle, St Beuno, was on hand to perform a miracle, and the girl's head was soon re-attached and she continued to live a long life of piety.

It is possible that the spring was sacred even before the coming of Christianity, but what is certain is that the waters have been recorded as bringing about miraculous cures since the twelfth century. By 1500, when the beautiful Gothic building was erected over the spring, St Winefride's had become one of the most celebrated shrines in the British Isles.

It is significant that St Winefride's survived the Dissolution of the Monasteries, carried out during the reign of Henry VIII. As part of this campaign, places of pilgrimage were ruthlessly put down – yet Holywell remained untouched. Indeed there is evidence that the Catholic mass continued to be said here even in times when Catholicism was outlawed.

According to an expert on the well, historian Tristan Gray Hulse, who lives in Denbighshire, there is a tradition that Henry's father, Henry VII, was cured at the well as a young boy. Henry VII's mother, Margaret, certainly had a passion for St Winefride's. This royal connection may be the reason it was spared.

Today pilgrims as well as tourists still visit St Winefride's Well, and this has earned it the name 'the Lourdes of Wales'. Actually, this is rather unfair – Lourdes has only been a place of pilgrimage since the nineteenth century, while St Winefride's has been so since at least the eleventh century!

There used to be many other healing and holy wells in Wales, but most are now sunk into obscurity. One such is Ffynnon Tegla (*ffynnon:* well) at Llandegla, between Ruthin and Wrexham. Today it is no more than a small, unregarded basin in the muddy margins of a farm track, but for centuries it was famous for its alleged ability to cure epilepsy.

The ceremony to effect this cure was elaborate and strange. It involved transferring the disease to live chickens. These were sold and subsequently looked after by St Tegla's Church in the village. The ceremony is described as follows:

'The patient repairs to the well after sunset, and washes himself in it; then, having made an offering by throwing into the water fourpence, he walks round it three times, and thrice recites the Lord's Prayer. If of the male sex, he offers a cock; if a woman, a hen.

'The bird is carried in a basket, first round the well, then round the church, and the rite of repeating the Pater Noster again performed. After all this, he enters the church, creeps under the altar, and making the Bible his pillow and the communion cloth his coverlet, remains there until the break of day.

'In the morning, having made a further offering of sixpence, he leaves the cock (or hen, as the case may be) and departs. Should the bird die, it is supposed that the disease has been transferred to it, and the man or woman consequently cured.'

The origin of this ceremony is obscure. Its implication of animal sacrifice is intriguing and hints at a great antiquity. The rite was continued into comparatively recent times, however. In 1855 the parish clerk of Llandegla said that an old man he knew 'remembered quite well seeing the birds staggering about from the effects of the fits' which had been transferred to them.

Ffynnon Sara can be found down a quiet country lane between Ruthin and Caerrigydrudion. Protected by a grove of spruce and holly trees, this healing well is a wonderfully serene place.

A 'bath' of stone, wide enough and deep enough to hold two or three people, runs off into a charming little stream, the banks of which, in spring, are clustered with violets and primroses. A few crude steps lead down into the water, which today is rather green and uninviting, but in past times was resorted to by many for its allegedly health-giving properties.

Tradition has it that Ffynnon Sara is named after a white witch who tended the well. It is said Sara lived in a nearby cottage, the ruins of which can be seen in the adjacent undergrowth. In Sara's day the cottage was crammed with discarded crutches and Bath chairs, left behind by those whom the well's water had cured.

This is a pretty story, but historians consider it more likely that 'Sara' is a corruption of Saeron, St Saeron being an Irish saint who was active in Denbighshire many centuries ago.

The condition of the well today, and the particular charm of its setting, is due to the attentions of a Victorian clergyman, the Rev. Percy Cook. Rev. Cook found the well derelict but he had the basin cleaned out, the grounds tidied and saw to the planting of the little grove of trees which now surrounds it.

Sources: *Welsh Folklore and Folk Custom* by T Gwynn Jones; Tristan Gray-Hulse; *Welsh Folklore* by Elias Owen; the November, 1985, edition of *Country Quest*. See plates 24, 25 and 26.

Christmas customs

In Wales it's not only the places that are curious – many old Welsh customs are very curious, too.

The most unusual customs took place at the great festivals of the year, particularly at Christmas and New Year. Perhaps the oddest was that of the Mari Lwyd, or Grey Mare. This was a grotesque creation, a horse's skull attached to a pole and draped in white cloth ,under which a young man would hide.The Mari Lwyd, accompanied by a party of men, often with blacked-up faces, would parade through the parish, and the youth controlling the monstrous hobby-horse would swoop on young women, using a wire to make the skull snap alarmingly.

The appearance of the Mari Lwyd was believed to bring luck to the community and, if nothing else, brought plenty of beer for the performers. The strange ritual is popularly believed to be related to pre-Christian fertility rites, but its precise origin and meaning is lost.

Also thought to be linked to the pagan past was another gruesome custom called the Hunting of the Wren.The poor little bird would be hunted high and low by boys and young men and would be killed with stones.The pathetic body was then placed in a wickerwork cage and carried round the houses.Again it was considered to bring luck – or rather bad luck to those who did not reward the youths with ale and treats.

Inarguably Christian is the custom of Plygain, a service held in church in the small hours of Christmas morning, and continued until dawn. Carols would be sung to greet the rising of the sun on this most special of days, and the congregation would then troop home, tired but happy. This custom has seen something of a revival in recent years.

In some houses in Wales the breakfast table would be set for two late on Christmas Eve, so that Mary and Joseph would be sure to find a welcome.

Apart from the poor wren, animals were well looked after on Welsh farms at Christmas – they all got a day off work and were fed on the very best fodder which could be found for them. This was due to the beasts' role in the Nativity, and it was said that if anyone settled down in the shippon on Christmas Eve, they would be sure to hear the animals talking – the one night of the year when they are able to do so.

Sources: The 1877, 1885, 1887, 1895 and 1897 volumes of Bye-gones.

An end and a beginning

Like Christmas, there are many strange rituals associated with New Year. It's a natural thing to wish to celebrate the birth of a new year, to put old troubles behind and to look with optimism to what the next twelve months may bring.

In northern Wales it was believed that suffering a disappointment on New Year's Day would lead to that person suffering disappointments throughout the year. It was considered very important throughout Wales to start off the year well.

One custom was that of making a 'clennig' or 'calennig', an assemblage of fruit and foliage which youngsters would take around the parish, collecting pennies for their trouble. Here is an 1894 description of the clennig:

'Children obtain an apple, stick into it three skewers tripod-wise, and a fourth to serve as a handle; and stud it with oats and raisins, whilst the whole is well-powdered with wheaten flour and the prominent parts are touched with gold-leaf, and on the top of the apple are stuck sprigs of box and rosemary, and on the ends of the leaves half-cracked hazel-nuts, so that the shells would clasp the foliage.'

The old custom still survives in parts of Wales. It also survives in the form of the Christingle, a similar creation, but with an orange being more often used than an apple. There are many suggestions as to meaning and origin of the clennig or Christingle, but nobody really knows for sure.

In some parts of Wales children would fill a jug from the nearest well at dawn and then sprinkle 'New Year's Rain' on everyone they met, or on the doors of those houses where no one was yet awake. Intriguingly, in some far eastern countries such as Thailand a very similar custom is carried out. On their New Year's Day (in April) the entire community will douse each other in water – although in a rather more boisterous fashion than the gentle sprinkling that occurs in Wales.

Just as in some houses the breakfast table was laid on Christmas Eve as a welcome for Mary and Joseph, at house in Trefeglwys, Powys, it was once the custom on Old New Year's Day to lay the table 'in honour of the reappearance of the sun'. The house stood at the foot of a hill and was in almost permanent shadow during the winter.

Today most of these old traditions have fallen out of use. But people still like to celebrate on New Year's Eve. For example, there are often as many merry-makers (per square metre) in St Peter's Square in Ruthin as there are in Piccadilly Circus in London.

Sources: The 1888, 1894, 1897 and 1901 volumes of *Bye-gones*. The complete extracts, and those of Christmas customs, can be found in full, with additions, in my own *Bye-gones* book, published in 1992.

The cuckoo's call

Along with the longer days and the flowers in the hedgerows, one of the harbingers of spring is the cuckoo. *The Times* newspaper has famously challenged readers for many years to write in as soon as they hear its call.

Although its familiar voice is welcomed, the cuckoo is a strange bird and has many odd beliefs associated with it. Everyone knows, of course, that it has the unpleasant habit of laying its eggs in other birds' nests so that its young will be reared without any effort of its own, and that once hatched its fledgling will push out the legitimate eggs to make sure it gets all the food for itself. But the bird takes on an almost otherworldly character in folklore, perhaps because it is heard so much more often than it is seen.

When the Welsh folklorist Elias Owen visited a sick old friend in the spring of 1895, he was asked: 'Have you heard the cuckoo?' Owen replied that he had, and his friend continued: 'I heard that he was about, and I was determined I would not hear him lying on the couch, so I got up and tidied myself, and went out and stood in the front, and I heard him in the wood over yonder, and now I shall not lie on this couch all the year through.'

The man's belief was that because he had heard the cuckoo's call he would not only get better, but would also be free of illness for the next twelve months. Owen added he had heard a few years previously of a young man who had been very ill and who had attempted to leave his sick bed to hear the cuckoo, but had been unable to – and he had died.

In old Caernarfonshire it was customary for old people

to kiss their hands when they first heard the cuckoo and ask: 'Cuckoo, cuckoo, how long shall I live?' Young people, more cheerfully, would ask 'When shall I marry?' The number of times the bird then sang 'cuckoo' would indicate the number of years.

People used to believe that anyone suffering from lumbago and rheumatism could cure themselves of their affliction by throwing themselves on the grass and rolling around three times as soon as they first heard the cuckoo's call. Of course, they might put their back out in the process! Another odd belief was that if the cuckoo's call was heard to 'stammer' during the night, there was bound to be rain the next day. It was also said that should you happen to hear a cuckoo before you'd breakfasted, it was an omen of coming misfortune. Generally, though, the cuckoo was seen – or rather heard – as a fortunate bird. If a miner heard the cuckoo's call for the first time on his way to work, he would immediately turn back and tell the colliery manager of the fact – and a holiday would be declared in celebration. Then they would all repair to the local pub to 'Wet the Cuckoo'.

Unfortunately, this cheerful custom began to die out in the 1860s. Wouldn't it be great if it was revived?

Source: *Bye-gones* volumes from 1894-7, also 1898-9 and 1901 and 1912.

Bride or bribe?

Ordinary couples once had to go through quite a trial just to get married in Wales. There were some surprising customs associated with the nuptials – customs whose intention seemed solely to extort money from the newlyweds.

The young couple and their guests might find themselves stopped on their way home from church with demands of money. Take this example from 1904, which was described at the time as being typical of what used to go on in Montgomeryshire:

'When the wedding party were driving from church, a number of the bridegroom's friends secured a strong rope, which they stretched across the road, and stopped the carriage, until they had been rewarded with a 'tip'. This occurred at two or three points of the road, on the journey from church.'

Some friends! A more violent version of the above involved 'chaining' or 'roping' the newly wedded pair. Once upon a time this might have been intended as a fun way of showing that the couple were now bound together, but it appears to have soon descended into another way to get money out of the couple. At any rate, the procedure could become violent, as evinced by an assault case brought by a young woman at Caerleon police court, Monmouthshire:

'Rachel Roderick, the bride, told the magistrates that . . . whilst she and her husband were going home they were confronted by a small knot of people who, with ropes in their hands, had gathered together for the purpose of carrying out the old custom of 'chaining'.

'The bride and bridegroom, wishing to escape this ordeal, sought shelter in a relation's house, but the husband eventually decided to make an attempt to proceed home. He was promptly stopped, however, before proceeding far and, as alleged, was bound hand and foot. The bride thereupon ran to his assistance and she was also bound.'

Another strange custom, but this time one which favoured the bride, involved her hiding somewhere in her parents' house on the morning of the wedding. Her bridegroom and his friends then had to search for her. A lot was at stake – if the men were unable to find the woman, the wedding would be postponed. The whole thing smacks of ancient tribal traditions in which young women were 'stolen' from their families.

In 1886, a writer recalled a particularly cunning example of hiding the bride, which nearly defeated the detective powers of the chagrined groom and his friends. They had searched all over the house; even the oven and the chimney had been explored, but in vain. As the laughter of the bride's friends redoubled, one keen-eyed lad suddenly noticed an area of wallpaper which was of a slightly different shade to the rest. He put his hand on it – it was wet! The story concludes:

'With a whoop of triumph he took out his jack-knife, ran it round the hidden door which had been pasted over an hour previously, and discovered the bride seated comfortably within, but almost choked with suppressed laughter.'

Sources: The 1885, 1886, 1904 and 1907 volumes of *Bye-gones*.

Pagan to Christian

The early missionaries to Britain found it difficult to convert the pagan populace to Christianity. Recognising this, the seventh century Pope Gregory stated:

'I have come to the conclusion that the temples of the idols in England should not on any account be destroyed. [Bishop] Augustine must smash the idols, but the temples themselves should be sprinkled with holy water and altars set up in them in which relics are to be enclosed. For we ought to take advantage of well-built temples by purifying them from devil-worship and dedicating them to the service of the true God.'

For England one can often, of course, also read Wales – but in this case this is particularly true, as Wales was more remote and the people more likely to retain their age-old religion. Gregory's edict may be the reason why so many churches appear to have been built on or in pre-Christian sacred sites.

An excellent example is the parish church of Corwen, in Denbighsire. A prehistoric standing stone has actually been incorporated into the wall of the church, which strongly suggests the site was a ritual centre in pre-Christian times. This five-foot high monolith rejoices under the name of Carreg y Big yn y Fach Rewllyd *('the pointed stone in the icy nook')* and stands surrounded by masonry near the east door.

Nearby, a slab of stone can be found featuring 'cup markings', little impressions believed to have been of ritual significance during the Bronze Age. This slab now forms the base of a medieval cross. As late as the eighteenth century the slab was itself supported by four or five other stones, so that it appears to have been a small cromlech, or burial chamber.

The church is situated on a rise above the town, in the place where, according to legend, some supernatural agency forced the builders to erect it, despite their original wish to site it elsewhere. It is also of interest that the name 'Corwen' can be translated as 'Sacred Circle' – perhaps the entire site was once ringed by a stone circle.

Another interesting churchyard is that at Gwytherin, in Conwy. As at Corwen, Gwytherin churchyard is situated on a prominent mound in the centre of the village and it too boasts standing stones – four of them in total. The Four Stones of Gwytherin are only three or four foot high, but they are interesting because they are arranged in a line. Prehistoric stone rows like this are rare in Wales.

On the westernmost stone there is an inscription dating from the period of the Roman occupation. It reads: 'Vinnemagli fili Senemagli', which translates as 'Vinnemaglus, son of Senemaglus'. Why this person should be commemorated here is unknown. Nor is it known whether the stone was already in place when the message was made, or whether the stone was erected some time after the other three.

When self-styled 'Modern Antiquarian' Julian Cope visited Gwytherin a few years ago, he imagined the 'Vinne' he could read in the inscription referred to St Winefride, Santes Gwenfrewi in Welsh, for the church is dedicated her. In fact, St Winefride – she of Holywell's famous holy well – set up a religious community at Gwytherin back in the Dark Ages. The saint was originally buried here, but centuries later her bones were dug up and removed to Shrewsbury by relic-hungry monks.

Today Gwytherin is well worth a visit. It is an isolated little village, situated halfway between Llansannan and Llanrwst and accessible via the B5384. Its isolation has helped preserve an atmosphere of sanctity and tranquillity, which the mysterious stones only enhance.

Back in Denbighshire, between Corwen and Cynwyd, can be found Llangar, the church of the stag. This is another isolated spot, the reason for which is explained in the following legend.

It is said that the original builders of the church found that every morning the work they had done the previous day was demolished and that during the night the builders had the same dream – a voice in a shining light telling them: 'Seek the White Stag, build your church where you see Him.'

Convinced the original site they had chosen was cursed, they agreed to take note of the dream, and they trudged through the countryside until, as dusk was falling, they suddenly saw, haloed in light, a magnificent white stag standing on a rise above a place where Afon Alwen flows into Afon Dee. Here they built their church.

Unfortunately, this site was too remote from any very populated area to attract many parishioners, and by the nineteenth century Llangar had fallen largely into disrepair. However, this means it escaped the attentions of the Victorian 'improvers' and – now beautifully restored – it is a snapshot of how a Welsh church would have looked two hundred years ago.

There is a gallery for musicians, enclosed pews and, most fascinating of all, numerous wall-paintings, including one of the fabled stag. The most striking is the mural facing the door. The first thing you see as you walk into the church is a life-size skeleton. Armed with pick and shovel, the tools of the gravedigger, and accompanied by an hourglass, this is a symbol of Death and a reminder of our brief span of years on this mortal earth.

Llangar church is now in the care of Cadw and open to the public by appointment only. When contacting Cadw, ask about visiting another nearby attraction – the exquisitely ornamented Rug chapel, on the same day.

Sources: *Old Stone Crosses of the Vale of Clwyd*, Elias Owen; *Prehistoric and Roman Remains in Denbighshire* by Ellis Davies; *Corwen and Its Neighbourhood* by Henry Roberts; *The Modern Antiquarian* by Julian Cope. See plates 20, 21 and 22.

Strange phenomena

Close encounters

UFO sightings are the stuff of science fiction and as such it would be reasonable to assume they are a modern phenomenon. But this is not necessarily the case. In Welsh folklore, for example, there are examples of 'tân-we', strange lights which would come down from the heavens and land near houses where people were soon to die.

For some time in the nineteenth and early twentieth centuries, Barmouth, in Gwynedd, was known for mysterious lights in the sky, what today we might call UFOs, but which the inhabitants at that time considered to be death omens, a kind of cannwyll corff or corpse candle.

In 1905 the phenomena took place during a religious revival in the region. Contemporary accounts refer to two different sightings which appeared to predict a death.

In the first case a party of people walking on the south side of the Mawddach estuary saw a strange light at the ferry-house of Penrhyn. One description has it that the light appeared to be inside the cottage and shining through the windows, the other describes it as being outside the house and similar to that produced by a bonfire. At any rate, the light had vanished by the time the witnesses reached the ferry-house. When they returned to Barmouth, they learnt that people there had seen the light, too. A few nights afterwards, the man who lived at the cottage fell into the water at high tide while stepping off a boat, and was drowned.

The second incident took place that same winter. Lights were seen dancing in the air by people on both banks of the estuary. At Borthwyn or Borthwnog – depending on which account you read – many people gathered to watch the lights. After a while all but one of the lights disappeared. This one descended to a little bay where boats were moored, and several men in a sloop which was anchored there also saw it. The light hovered over one particular boat and then vanished. Two or three days later the man to whom that boat belonged drowned in Barmouth harbour.

It is no wonder, then, that in the nineteenth century when some poachers in Buckley, Flintshire, saw what today we would call a UFO, they were afraid it would bring ill fortune down upon them. They were also afraid to talk about the sighting for fear of being imprisoned for trespassing, but sons and nephews of the witnesses told the story to Buckley historian the late James Bentley, who preserved this fascinating account for us.

A serious dispute over pay at Buckley colliery in the 1880s had led to the miners going on strike and they were forced to poach to feed their families. Unfortunately, all the land thereabouts belonged to the mine owners, which made the enterprise a very risky affair. One dark, moonless night, five companions crept down to the fields south of the town and set their traps and released a ferret.

'Everywhere was pitch black and deathly silent,' recounted Mr Bentley. 'Suddenly a feeling of electrical tension seemed to descend upon their crouching figures. They had the feeling of being observed. Glancing up, they all saw a large, purplish-red luminous ball hovering above them. Silently it descended into a field adjacent. Petrified, they cowered down into the hedgerow and covered their heads with nets.

'Then they sensed a lessening of tension and heard a

slight swishing sound. One of them cautiously opened his eyes and peered over the bank. A swirling ball of smoke, with small tongues of flame issuing from the base, was lifting off the ground.'

The men ran home in alarm and vowed each other to secrecy. The following evening one brave soul returned to collect the gear they had left behind in their panic.

'Peering into the nearby field, where the object had appeared, he saw a large brown ring – it was scorched grass.'

Equally interesting – and perhaps even more important to the student of such phenomena because the account is first-hand and contemporary rather than being recorded second-hand – is the record of UFOs which plagued a farmhouse near Pwllheli. These sightings took place even earlier than the Buckley case, in 1875 (more than a century before the term 'flying saucer' was used and predating by many years even the science fiction stories of H.G. Wells).

Mr Picton-Jones, of Yoke House, just inland from Bae Ceredigion (*Bae*: bay), wrote a letter to *The Field* describing some very strange things seen by his family: 'Some years ago we witnessed here what we have never seen before – certain lights, eight in number . . . moving in horizontal, perpendicular and zigzag directions. Sometimes they were of a light blue colour, then like the bright light of a carriage lamp, then almost like an electric light . . . '

Mr Picton-Jones and his family saw the lights regularly. The most dramatic encounter took place in late February, 1875. Here is an edited version of Mr Picton-Jones's own account:

'We saw twelve at the same time, two were very bright,

the one of a red, the other of a blue colour. It was a very dark and foggy night and my brother, my son Percy, my keeper and I went out about a mile to see if we could get near them. When we had gone about half a mile, we observed four or five behind us. One light that had appeared before we started seemed to go in, and out, round the corner, on to the cart horse stable, round its gable end, then on to the barn . . . '

He was mystified as to their origin, but presumed them to have some natural origin, perhaps some form of marsh gas or 'will-o'-the-wisp'. Perhaps it is just as well his family lived a century before 'alien abductions' had been heard of, or they would have been terrified.

Sources: *British Goblins* by Wirt Sikes; *A Book of South Wales* by Sabine Baring-Gould; Mr James Bentley; the 1905 and 1875 volumes of *Bye-gones*. See plate 19.

Dreams come true

The twin worlds of dreams and reality can sometimes overlap – with extraordinary results.

Take the case of a Mr Boardman, who was saved from certain death by a dream. Mr Boardman had been preaching one night in Mold (one year in the eighteenth century) and he was making his way across the Dee estuary when the tide came in more quickly than he had anticipated and he found himself in a very perilous position. The water had soon risen up to his knees, and he gave himself up as lost.

But then he perceived two men running down a hill and – to his joy – he saw them get into a boat. He was rescued! In the boat, his horse swimming by their side, Mr Boardman learnt the amazing facts of his deliverance. One of his rescuers told him:

'I dreamed I must get to the top of such a hill; when I awoke the dream made such an impression on me I could not rest. I went and called my friend, and desired him to accompany me. When we came to the place we saw nothing more than usual. However, I begged him to go with me to another hill, at a small distance, and there we saw your distressing situation.'

This remarkable story is not unique. Another case, narrated in the Proceedings of the Society for Psychical Research, is as follows:

About 1871, Miss Phillips of Church Street, Welshpool, had a deaf and dumb maid who fell ill and needed a change of air. Miss Phillips proposed to send her to her brother for three weeks but the girl was unwilling to go and, on the appointed morning, a Tuesday, she was nowhere to be seen.

The house was searched from the attic to the cellar, but she seemed to have vanished. Miss Phillips was very distressed.

On the following Friday (or possibly Wednesday) morning the superintendent of the police called and begged to be allowed to make a search of the house himself. Miss Phillips consented and Inspector Strefford, who had never been in the house before, walked straight to the door of the cellar stairs, and went down.

In the cellar they found the girl in an open flue directly beneath the fireplace in the room above. The opening from the flue to the cellar was not above eighteen inches high, and the girl had drawn some carpeting after her so as to conceal her legs. She was stuck fast and they had to get bricklayers' tools and dig out some bricks before they could get her out.

The unfortunate maid's deliverance from a horrible fate was also down to a dream. Inspector Strefford had awoken in the middle of the night and had told his wife: 'I know where that poor girl is. She is up a chimney in a cellar belonging to the house in which she lives.'

Afterwards, he felt compelled to go the house to test the truth of his dream – with the happy results just described.

Sources: The 1882 and 1909 volumes of *Bye-gones*.

In the dark

I spend a lot of time looking through 'old volumes of forgotten lore', as Poe has it. Among the most fruitful sources for folk belief and strange stories are old periodicals. These include the journals of antiquarian and field club societies; even the august *Archaeologia Cambrensis* boasts a fair few ghost stories and legends.

My favourite of the lot is *Bye-gones*, which ran from 1871 to 1939. Its volumes are packed full of interesting stuff relating to Wales and the border counties and many of the scraps of folklore and old legends contained within its pages are to be found nowhere else – they were collected by enthusiasts, sent in and never published again. Even Elias Owen, author of *Welsh Folklore*, contributed items (under the byline 'E.O.') which never made it into his book, and he continued to make contributions after the book was published.

So enamoured of *Bye-gones* was I that I edited a collection of some of my favourite items, which was published by Gwasg Carreg Gwalch in 1992. Many of the stories in *Wales of the Unexpected* have come from *Bye-gones* (such as the *Dream come true* tales above). Here are two more bizarre stories:

A former rector of Llangadfan, Powys, recalled an amusing yarn about an 'innocent' (i.e. naive or dim-witted) family of Cwmllecoediog, Garthbeibio.

He writes: 'Whilst they were all in bed one dark winter night, a number of mischievous youths walled up the windows of the house with sods, so that not a ray of light could enter in when daylight made its appearance. The family slept comfortably for the night, and the whole of the next day; but on the evening of the second day they began to think that it was the longest night that ever existed since "darkness was on the face of the deep".

'They began to become uneasy, and they resolved to get up to look for the sun. The old man called upon the lads to follow him, saying: "We must go and look for the sun." And away they went, and made diligent search for it without any success, until they arrived at the summit of Bwlch-y-fedwen; here daylight greeted them, to their great joy.

'The old worthy of Cwmllecoediog was ever afterwards known by the dignified title of the "man of light".'

Equally perplexed were the Ffoulkes family of Llandrillo, Denbighshire. They awoke one morning to find their home had been transported to a strange place. Their story was recounted to a *Bye-gones* correspondent by his grandmother, who was presumably one of the family members at the time. The incident took place about the year 1809 – if it took place at all.

Speaking of his grandmother, the *Bye-gones* correspondent writes: 'Her father and mother and family had retired for the night, and on awakening in the morning and looking out through the window, were utterly bewildered, not knowing the locality they were in, and after looking around and finding the dwelling house and outbuildings to be the same, they all came to the conclusion that the fairies had carried their house to some strange place.

'On the neighbours from Llandrillo arriving, they found that an avalanche had taken the whole buildings and carried them down the slope of the mountain until they rested upon a flat surface and with great difficulty they were rescued from their perilous position, not one having been disturbed in the night, the avalanche having surrounded the buildings and carried them safely down.'

Sources: The 1894 and 1895 volumes of *Bye-gones*.

Old flames

Recent winters in Wales have been fairly mild, but nature was not so kind in the year 1773. Not only did those in northern Wales have to suffer dreadful blizzards and giant drifts of snow, they also had to contend with – a volcano!

This, at least, was the information given out by that year's *Annual Register*, a record of significant events published in London. The 1773 edition quotes the following letter, headed 'Holywell, Flintshire, February 2':

'The memory of man cannot recollect such quantities of snow to have fallen in these parts, as last week; my house is three stories high, and I can hardly lay me down in security in the garrett. Men, women, and children, and cattle, have found their tombs in the snow.

'The night before last, Moelfamma (a high mountain in this neighbourhood) was heard to utter, as it were, deep groans; the adjacent hills trembled from their roots. The noise at eleven o'clock was like the sound of a distant thunder, from the rolling of huge stones down a craggy precipice.

'At twelve there was a loud clap, and the vortex of the hill threw up in the same instance vast bodies of combustible matter; liquid fire rolled amongst the heaps of ruins; at the close of all, nature seemed to make a grand effort, and rent one side of the mountain, which was solid stone, into an hiatus . . . the summit of the hill tumbled into this vast opening; and the top appears level, which before was almost perpendicular.'

This fantastic tale is just that – fantastic. The letter was a hoax; there was no eruption. Moel Fama, highest of the

Clwydian Range, is an inert lump of shale and has never been a volcano. However, for the yarn to have been believed, it just shows how wild Wild Wales seemed to distant Londoners two centuries ago.

In contrast, however, there appears to have been no hoax behind the odd phenomenon which caused havoc to the residents of Harlech nearly a hundred years before the 'volcano'.

In the year 1694 a 'pestilential vapour resembling a pale blue flame' rose out of a marshy area of coastline called Morfa Bychan. The luminous blanket was eight miles wide and drifted over fields and houses until it settled on Harlech town. Apparently it set light to sixteen hay-ricks and two barns on its journey and any animals, such as sheep and cows, which browsed on the grass over which it had passed were poisoned and fell dead. Oddly, however, human beings seemed to remain unaffected.

The mysterious vapour only travelled at night. For some unexplained reason it could be dissipated by creating loud sounds. In time it evaporated of its own accord but returned the following summer, though in a lesser quantity and with less destructive power than before.

No credible explanation has ever been put forward for the nature of the 'Harlech Vapour'; a contemporary suggestion that it was caused by the decay of a swarm of 'locusts' near Aberdaron seems unlikely.

Sources: Moel Fama eruption from the 1877 and 1885 volumes of *Bye-gones*; Harlech Vapour from *A Description of Caernarvonshire* by Edmund Hyde-Hall. See plate 7.

Stories from my readers

Readers write in

The most enjoyable thing about writing the *Wales of the Unexpected* column is that so many readers wrote back – telling of their own experiences with the supernatural in Wales.

Mr Peter Morris, JP, wrote to tell me about a ghost he saw at Trefor, on Llŷn. The sighting took place some years ago, it would seem, when Mr Morris worked in London (he now lives near Pwllheli).

Mr Morris had booked a week's holiday in a terraced cottage in the village of Trefor. He was delighted with the accommodation, unaware that it had an unexpected occupant. 'One night,' he wrote, 'I was wakened by a small noise to find a lady dressed in the style of the 1800s standing by the side of the bed between me and the door. After a few moments she vanished.'

So as not to alarm his family, Mr Morris kept the incident to himself. Some years later, back at his desk in London, he was reminded of the ghost when one of his staff mentioned that relatives had dined with him the night before and when he had mentioned 'his boss', his daughter-in-law had asked: 'Is that the chap who stayed in the haunted house in our village?'

Naturally, Mr Morris now wanted more details. His colleague promised to get them, if he could, from his daughter-in-law, and the following story emerged. The woman's grandmother had told her that many years ago the house had been one 'of ill repute' and that a fight had taken place there over a girl. A local lad killed an Irish sailor. Strangely, it is the girl who haunts the house, rather than the murdered sailor.

Equally interesting, but with an origin as yet undiscovered, is the ghost seen by Mrs Hignett, of Colwyn Bay, when she and her husband took over the running of the Red Lion pub in Llansannan in 1983. They were aware of an eerie presence and became used to hearing mysterious footsteps. Then, one day when Mrs Hignett was alone in the pub, she thought she heard someone enter the snug, and went to investigate.

'There was a man in a black coat, collar up to his eyes, and with a black hat standing at the end of the bar,' she wrote. 'He was there for a few seconds and then went. I thought he looked like one of the Roundheads or similar. I later found out there had been a staircase where I had seen the person.'

Oddly enough, that same weekend an American tourist saw an apparition – perhaps the same apparition – in the pub opposite. Mrs Hignett thought it better to keep quiet about her ghost: 'People would have thought I was cashing in, so to speak.'

I don't believe that the ghost has been seen again, in either pub. Perhaps he, too, was a tourist – from the Twilight Zone.

Not all ghosts are visible. Many of us have been disturbed at some time in our lives by that mysterious phenomenon known as 'things that go bump in the night'. Ghosts, unlike good little children, are often heard but not seen.

The 'rattling of chains' which accompanies apparitions in old stories first appeared in writings dating from Roman times. Unexplainable taps, knocks, bashes, crashes, scratchings and scrapings form a part of many hauntings today.

A reader told me of a haunted room in a house near Caernarfon in which weird scratchings were often heard on the wooden partition dividing it from the room next door. This gentleman's aunt, who slept in the latter chamber, would often hear the sound at night. On one occasion, she was in the haunted room, fetching some things out of a wardrobe, when she was startled by 'a terrible sound as if a whole tray of crockery had been dropped. There was no visible sign of anything'.

Other readers wrote about visions they have had of recently departed pets, in response to my column on that subject. Rowland Roberts, of Beaumaris, wrote that he saw his deceased Jack Russell, Shon, standing in the doorway of his bedroom, as if waiting to be taken for a walk, as she used to do in life. She vanished almost before he had time to register she was there.

Mr and Mrs Kingslaid, of Llangollen, were also visited by a pet dog some little while after it had passed away. The couple were very upset after Pinky, the younger of two Yorkshire terriers they owned (the other, of course, was named Perky) unexpectedly died. The next day, Mrs Kingslaid walked into the living room, where her husband was sitting on the sofa, and Perky was in a bean bag. Then she saw something incredible.

As calmly as she could, she asked her husband to look at the bean bag and to tell her what he saw. Bursting into tears, he said: 'Pinky is in the bean bag with Perky.'

Mrs Kingslaid reported that 'a few minutes later, Pinky had gone – so at least she came to say she was still around. Even to this day we still shed a tear when we remember it.'

The ghost at the crossroads

Crossroads, bridges and stiles were all once considered eerie after dark because they were things which connected places together rather than being actual places themselves. They were shadowy, otherworldly.

Crossroads were particularly sinister because they were once traditional places to bury suicides. In unenlightened days those who had taken their own lives were thought unfit for burial on holy ground. It was also popular belief that the spirits of suicides were likely to be especially troubled, and were unlikely to rest easy in their graves. It was hoped that a spirit materialising at a crossroads would become confused, trapped even, by the number of lanes meeting there.

Mr John Roberts, of Brynteg, encountered one such apparition one winter's twilight, at Hafod Onnen crossroads, near Rhosgoch on Anglesey. He had been out shooting with his friend Ted. As twilight descended, Ted shot a pheasant, but it was only wounded and ran off into the gloom. Of course, it is very wrong to leave a wounded bird to suffer, so Ted was anxious to recover it.

Ted suggested that Mr Roberts should return to his van while he searched for the bird, and he did so. It was then that he saw the ghost. Mr Roberts takes up the story:

'By now it was dark, and as I walked toward the Hafod Onnen Crossroads, I was approached by a tall man similar to Ted. Taking it for granted that it was Ted, I asked him "Did you get the bird?" No reply. "Where's the dog?" No reply. "Where's your gun?" No reply.

'I followed him, almost touching him, but he kept out of

reach. He was wearing a full-size oilskin coat, and as I was about to touch him he disappeared through a gate that was locked. Had he been a real man, the sheep in the field would have automatically come running for feed, as there was a trough by the gate. But they didn't.'

In fact, the tall dark stranger had vanished completely. Anxious, no doubt, to be sure he hadn't imagined the apparition, Mr Roberts asked around the neighbourhood to find out whether there had been any previous sightings. He discovered that 'the Hafod Onnen Ghost was always well known'.

Two black dogs and a haunted wood

Mr William Owen, of Porthmadog, kindly wrote about the strange experience of his late father, which took place sometime between the years 1910 and 1915 when he was a young man. It was dusk and he was cycling down a lane near Llanfechell in the north of Anglesey when he caught sight of a black dog a few yards ahead of him.

'From all accounts,' writes Mr Owen, 'it was a fierce-looking creature the size of a calf. It did not venture to attack in any way but it was just following my father like a shadow. However fast my father rode his bike, the dog managed to keep a few yards ahead. When they came to the junction of the Cemaes Bay to Holyhead road it simply vanished!'

As indicated earlier (see page 18) the Black Dog – or Gwyllgi as it is known in Wales – is a popular figure in old Welsh ghostlore and I was fascinated to learn of this more recent sighting of such a spectre. Nor was it the only one. A week or two later, Mrs Jones-Williams, of Llangefni, wrote about another Anglesey Gwyllgi.

When her late husband was a little boy about seventy years ago, he and his father were walking down a path near Llanfachraeth, Anglesey, when they were frightened by 'a big Black Dog' which 'vanished into thin air'. The scene was a footpath which runs through a farm called Dronwy.

Mrs Jones-Williams was brought up in Trofarth, near Abergele. When she was a child, she was told by her mother that a woman had been murdered many years previously, and that her body had been dumped in a deep, dark dingle called Nant Dywyll. Moreover, 'the body was seen walking about at night'.

'I wouldn't go near there in the daylight, let alone at night,' said Mrs Jones-Williams, but she added: 'It might have been a story to keep the kids out of the woods – and it sure did.'

See plate 31.

Weird Wrexham

I received several stories about ghosts in the Wrexham area, a well-populated bit of Wales but one with many unexpectedly rural corners in among the housing estates and business parks.

Dr Stan Morton reported that when he lived as a child at Ruabon, the grounds of the well-known Lindisfarne College with its distinctive column were considered very eerie. A raised pathway called Lady Harriet's Walk was said to be patrolled by the ghost of a woman – presumably Lady Harriet herself.

Many years ago a teacher at Ruabon High School set her English class the task of finding local ghost stories and writing them up for homework. The Lindisfarne column featured in many of those the children collected, perhaps because it is such an important local landmark. It should be remembered that the former college started life as Wynnstay Hall, a very important manor house.

One of the stories featured the aforementioned Lady Harriett. According to this tale, Lady Harriett climbed the tower so she could watch a fox-hunt, but she fell off – and was trampled by all the horses racing by. The most bizarre legend of the column included a strange ritual with a very unexpected result. One child wrote:

'On a certain day at 12 o'clock midnight with full moon weird things happen. Some people say if you go round [the column] ten times and knock on the door a woman with an axe is supposed to chase you into the woods.'

Mrs Phyllis Lister, of Brymbo, had an eerie experience in St Giles's Parish Church in Wrexham. Mrs Lister, who used to work as a guide in the grand old building, says: 'I have heard some very strange noises in the church and footsteps walking down the aisle. I had someone with me later and she heard the footsteps, too.'

Mrs Lister also reported that Thomas Telford's famous aqueduct at Pontcysyllte is said to be haunted by the ghost of a woman. Her identity is a mystery.

Some years ago, I heard that the aqueduct is haunted by the spirits of the men who died in accidents during its construction. A similar explanation may account for the apparition of a miner which Mrs Lister says has been glimpsed near the Miner's Institute in Gresford – the Gresford Disaster was one of the worst mining accidents of the twentieth century.

Another reader, a gentleman living at Coed-poeth, reported that a friend of his saw a ghost one moonlit night by the stone bridge at nearby Nant Mill. A man in a bowler hat walked past him – and then vanished.

58. Small spirits

Many people think that if they ever saw a ghost they would be terrified. This is often not the case. Most witnesses describe ghosts as very benign apparitions of very ordinary looking people. Many are the ghosts of children.

Two readers from the Wrexham area described ghosts of children they had seen.

Linda Stocker saw an apparition about fifteen years ago in a farmhouse near Coed-poeth. Mrs Stocker explained that a tiny old cottage had stood beside this farmhouse for many years and had recently been knocked down to create an extension. Once when Mrs Stocker visited her friends at the farmhouse, she had occasion to go upstairs and it was then that she was surprised to see a little girl skipping happily along a corridor.

The girl was wearing a long dark dress and a big floppy hat. She looked to be about ten years old. Mrs Stocker hardly had time to register the girl's appearance before she had skipped into the part of the building that had once belonged to the old cottage – and there vanished. Mrs Stocker hurriedly followed but – rather as she had expected – the girl was nowhere to be seen. She was in no doubt she had seen a ghost. So as not to alarm them, she decided against mentioning her experience to her friends.

She did mention it, however, to an elderly woman who lived in the village, in the hope of finding some clue as to the ghost's origin.

'My friend told me that when she was a little girl herself – about seventy years ago – she had known the family who'd lived in the cottage,' said Mrs Stocker. 'She recalled they had had a daughter who had died there when still a child and my friend felt certain that it was her ghost I had seen.'

An even spookier story was recounted by Anna Bayley, a young woman of twenty-three who lives at Pen-y-cae. The ghost child she encountered was very real to her – but then she was also very young.

She wrote: 'When I was a child I used to have visits from a young boy every night. He wore the old blue and white stripey pyjamas and the floppy hat and I have always remembered how red his lips were – I can still see his face to this day!

'Unfortunately, I cannot remember what we talked about, but after we had finished talking he got into bed with me and we went to sleep. At the time I was not scared but the next morning I would cry to my mum and be dreading bed time.'

Anna added: 'This went on for about six years and then all of a sudden it stopped and I have never seen him again.'

The man in 'fancy dress'

Contrary to popular belief, many ghosts are seen in broad daylight. Mr A.N. Foulkes saw a very peaceful phantom one bright June day, while riding down a lane near Llansantffraid Glan Conwy. Peaceful though it was, it startled Mr Foulkes's horse. The animal reared up and nearly dismounted Mr Foulkes, who, on calming it down, then looked to see what had upset it.

Coming up the lane towards them was a man 'in fancy dress'. He was wearing 'a large chocolate-brown hat with a wide brim and a rounded middle like a bowler' and 'a pale shirt' over which was 'a smock coat which was pale brown'. Only the top half of the figure was visible over the hedge, but Mr Foulkes got the impression he was jogging along slowly on a horse-drawn cart.

'His head was over on one side as if he was dozing'. As he reached a corner below, the man became obscured from view and Mr Foulkes's agitated horse suddenly relaxed. Mr Foulkes trotted down the lane, expecting to meet the strange individual – but he had vanished.

It was then that Mr Foulkes got the eerie feeling that he had seen something unearthly. Chats with elderly people strongly suggested he had seen the apparition of a farmer named Wynne who had been known to return somewhat drunk from market, fast asleep on his cart while his patient horse pulled him up the lane.

Needless to say, Mr Wynne had been dead for very many years.

The man in the brown coat

Mrs Weatherall, of Colwyn Bay, wrote to tell of a ghost she saw near her former home on Anglesey.

One evening in 1981, she was driving back to Llanfechell, when she saw a man crossing the road ahead of her. Her husband, who was in the passenger seat, couldn't see the man and asked why she had suddenly slowed down. Mrs Weatherall watched in amazement as the figure calmly walked through the solid wall of a cottage facing the road.

Mrs Weatherall describes the figure as 'wearing a knee-length brownish coat, some sort of hat, and he walked with the slow, steady gait of a countryman.' The cottage was one Mrs Weatherall had passed many times before.

A day or two later, Mrs Weatherall's husband was buying eggs from the people who lived opposite the cottage and rather humorously mentioned his wife's ghost. To his surprise, they confirmed that 'they saw him many times appearing through the wall and walking across the road, then vanishing'.

Mrs Weatherall herself discussed the ghost with an elderly friend, and this lady felt sure the apparition was that of a miller who had lived in the cottage when she was a little girl, and who had gone insane. The blank wall he was seen to walk through was comparatively modern – in the miller's time it would have been a way round to the original door.

The High Street puritan

Apparitions can pop up in Wales at any time – even when you're doing your weekly shop.

Some years ago Mr and Mrs Johnson were in Bangor High Street, looking at the display in the window of a bookshop, when their eyes were drawn by an odd-looking character reflected in the glass. So prominent was he among the busy crowds of shoppers that they both turned round to watch him.

They wrote: 'Walking down the High Street towards the clock tower was a man dressed in Puritan clothes – tall black hat, a long-tailed black coat, high-buttoned black vest, a white collared shirt, knee-length black breeches with white stockings. He also wore black shoes with a buckle.'

One's first thought might be that the gentleman was taking part in some sort of pageant, but Mr and Mrs Johnson were struck by the fact that no one else seemed to see this outlandish figure; he didn't draw a single glance as he made his way through the crowds.

'At the time the High Street was very busy with pedestrians yet nobody except us seemed to see him,' they wrote. 'He did not walk through people but in a straight line and people did not seem to get in his way. We watched as he went out of view among the crowds.'

Not surprisingly, when the Johnsons entered the bookshop, it was a book on ghosts they chose to take home with them. What was a surprise, however, was that the book contained a story about a very similar apparition, a man in the dress of a Puritan of the seventeenth or eighteenth century and seen in an equally incongruous location – in this case the M6 service station at Keele. Mr and Mrs Johnson no longer have the book and were unable to recall its title, but I recognised it as *Ghosts Over Britain* by Peter Moss (published in 1977).

The Keele witness, Geoffrey Wright, told Peter Moss that the Puritan seemed real but no one else appeared to observe him and he mysteriously disappeared. Some months later Mr Wright saw the figure again, more than a hundred miles away from where he first saw him, walking down a busy street in Colchester. His description of this sighting strongly resembles that of the Puritan seen in Bangor:

'No one seemed to notice him, and though he did not appear to take any deliberate avoiding action he never seemed to get in anyone's way or to bump into anyone.'

Grave concerns

One black night in the middle of winter Mrs E. said farewell to her friend Mrs O., a widow who lived at the Chapel House in Llangaffo, Anglesey, and began to walk home. She was surprised to see a tall man approaching her through the gloom, apparently making his way to the Chapel House himself.

She said hello to the man, but received no reply. Mrs E. felt some concern that this surly individual should be making his way to her elderly friend's house. It was too dark for her to see the man's face, but he was very tall and appeared to be dressed in black, with a long overcoat down to the ground. On his head was a top hat – an item of apparel which probably hadn't been seen in Llangaffo for something like a hundred years.

Mrs E. watched as the stranger continued on his way to the Chapel House. He did not call at the house, however, but skirted it and stepped onto the gravel path which led to the cemetery. His feet made no sound on the gravel. Soon the darkness of the surrounding trees swallowed him up and Mrs E. saw him no more.

After Mrs E. had told Mrs O. about what she had seen, they both agreed that the figure had probably been no living man, but a ghost. Chatting among their friends, they learnt that the person who lived at the Church House at the opposite end of the village had also seen the mysterious man in black. He would emerge from the churchyard in the middle of the night and silently make his way to the chapel's burial ground.

Now a theory emerged as to who this ghost might be. It

seems that in 1895 a man named Pritchard died in Llangaffo. Mr Pritchard was a staunch chapel-goer with a strong antipathy towards the established church. He stated that he did not wish to be buried in the churchyard, but this wish was ignored on his death. With no chapel cemetery then in existence, there was nowhere other than the churchyard to bury him.

Is the apparition that of Mr Pritchard? Is his spirit so angry at being buried in church ground that every night it makes its way to the chapel cemetery, seeking the rest that was denied it? Mrs E., Mrs O. and her friends believed so.

Note: The reader and her friend both wished to remain anonymous.

The lady in the lake

A 'Mrs G.' – who does not wish her full name to be printed – saw a ghost one dark night when she was a teenager. Here is her story:

'It was winter, 1940, I was eighteen years old. The Second World War was on, and, of course, the hated blackout – no light on in the streets or to be seen through any windows from the outside.

'I lived in the village of Pen-y-groes, near Caernarfon. My friend and myself were shop assistants. My friend lived in the village of Tal-y-sarn about a mile away. The shop closed at 7pm. There was nothing to do in the village – there was a cinema, but by the time we finished work, it was too late to visit, so to pass a couple of hours, I would accompany my friend home, going along the bottom road to Tal-y-sarn, and coming home along the old road about the last half mile on my own after seeing my friend home.

'About half way, just before reaching a farm called Pant Du, I had to stop for a lady coming out before me from the gate. I can see her now – long black dress or coat, a white lace bonnet, red hair fringe along her forehead, and carrying a large shiny milk can. I could even see her shiny shoes. She walked slowly in front of me and up the little slope in the road.

'I suddenly realised – how was I able to see the old lady so plainly and yet I could hardly see my fingers in front of me, because of the dark night? I turned around to look after her, and I could see her before my eyes going smaller and smaller, until she somehow disappeared into the ground. It was then I realised I had seen a ghost.'

'Mrs G' later learnt that she was not the only person to have seen the apparition. Quite recently she spoke to a lady in her fifties who saw it in the same place on a winter's evening when she was taking a walk with her husband.

At the time of her own sighting, Mrs G. was told by a neighbour that a woman had been found drowned in a lake at the Pant Du farm, and it was popularly supposed to be this unfortunate person's spirit which haunted the lane.

What fascinates me about this sighting is the detail which struck 'Mrs G' herself as odd – that she could see the figure so clearly in the dark.

Ghosts encountered at night are often clearly visible. Perhaps they are being seen as the person would have been seen in life – going about their business in daylight. It's an interesting sidelight (if you'll pardon the pun) on the ghost experience.

More from Tal-y-sarn

Following on from Mrs G.'s letter, Mrs Jean MacDonald wrote from the Isle of Islay in Scotland to confirm that the ghost was well-known:

'I was brought up at Tal-y-sarn. As children we all knew the story of the woman who had drowned in the Pant Du Farm lake.'

Although Jean never saw the 'lady in the lake' herself, she did see another ghost at Tal-y-sarn. Here is her story:

'This happened in the early 1930s when I was about seven years of age. Dusk was falling one summer evening and my friend, aged about nine, and I were the only ones left at the 'Parc' [an area of rough ground used as a makeshift playground]. Both of us were kneeling on a grassy slope busily digging for 'pig-nuts' – these were part of the root system of a small white flower. They were good to eat and tasted rather peppery! I suddenly had a feeling that someone was watching me, so I looked up.

'Walking slowly along the path above me was a tall black man! He was dressed in black and had a white shirt and on his head he wore a tall black hat. I was very surprised as I had not encountered a black man before. He reached the stile which led to the path to Pant Du Farm; he stopped on the bottom step and turned around and smiled at us. Not a word was uttered. He then turned his back to us, climbed up to the top step and disappeared in front of my eyes.'

Neither girl admitted to the other that they had seen this 'apparition' but both made hurried excuses and headed to their homes. They never spoke about their experience until more than fifty years later. At the same time Jean learnt that on another occasion her two brothers had also seen the apparition, but at a different location. They and several other youths had been sitting on the steps of the Bont Ddu railway bridge when they saw the tall black man coming down the steps towards them ...

'He walked by them, then crossed over the road, stepped over the stile in to the field and disappeared as he was walking up the path. This path was at the bottom of the same field which led to the farm.'

Jean learnt then that the ghost was known by the name of 'Solomon'.

Who was Solomon? A black man living – and presumably dying – in a small Caernarfonshire village prior to the 1930s would have been fairly unusual, since most of the black population of Britain in those days was largely confined to the cities and ports. Perhaps, therefore, a local history society would be able to track down the true identity of this striking gentleman, and possibly find a link between him and the lady drowned in the lake ...

By the way, your house is haunted

Is it possible to live in a haunted house without ever experiencing the ghost? A reader wrote about a cottage he lived in for fifteen years without he, his wife, or his children ever seeing anything. Nevertheless his tale contains such an extraordinary twist – a coincidence which convinced him of the haunted nature of his home – that it deserves to be told.

The cottage has since been sold, so my correspondent has asked me to name neither himself nor the village where the cottage is situated. Here is his story in his own words:

'In 1987 my wife and I bought an old cottage in Llŷn and when we had settled in, invited my mother, who lived in Poole, Dorset, to come and stay with us. Our youngest son was away and she was to use his room.

'The morning after her first night she came downstairs in quite a subdued state and only after persistent questioning did she reveal the problem. She said that during the night she had been awakened by a very old woman pulling at the duvet; the woman said something in Welsh and then disappeared. My mother was obviously very shaken and said that she would neither sleep in that room again nor stay in the cottage again, a promise which she kept.

'In 1991 my wife and I had to go to Birmingham for a couple of days on business and she arranged for a young lady friend to house sit. When we returned she said she had had a disturbing experience during the first night when she was awakened by someone pulling at the duvet. She woke to see a small, very old woman standing at the bottom of the bed. The woman said 'Everything is alright' in Welsh, then disappeared.

'Two years later, after an afternoon in Poole, we were returning home in a taxi when my mother commented to the driver that he didn't sound like a local man. He said that in fact he came from Manchester. My mother then asked him if he missed his home. He said no, but he did miss north Wales, where he spent regular holidays.

'I asked him where in north Wales he went to and to my surprise he said [my village]. He was equally surprised when I told him that I in fact lived there. I asked him where in the village he stayed and he named my cottage and when I told him that I owned that property he stopped the car in disbelief to talk to me.

'He then said: 'I'll tell you something, that cottage is haunted.'

'My mother gripped my arm and said: 'I told you so.'

'I asked the driver to continue and he claimed that his brother had been wakened in the night by a little old lady pulling at the bedclothes and that the experience was so frightening for him that he refused to return to the cottage again.'

Nightmare of a dream home

Among all the blurb that estate agents use to sell their over-priced houses, one thing they will not mention is whether or not it is haunted.

When Owena Thomas moved to a seaside village in Anglesey with her husband and three-year-old son some years ago, she immediately fell in love with an old white-washed cottage perched up on the cliff's edge, its garden romantically wild and overgrown. She was determined to buy it; it seemed the perfect home for her young family.

But she had no way of knowing that the charming old place was reputed to be badly haunted, that the path past it was avoided at night even by the coastguards and that the presence that possessed it would put her child's life in danger.

Sure enough, Owena got her wish and the Thomas's moved into the cottage on the cliff. At about the same time, royalties on her author husband's latest book allowed him to buy a boat and the family spent an idyllic summer, fishing out at sea, picnicking, catching crabs on the beach, and returning to their home, where Owena and her husband would sleep in a room which had once been a chapel – a room illuminated by a big stained-glass window.

The only hint that there was anything wrong with the cottage was that at times the living room was unbearably cold.

'I had never experienced such an icy chilliness as that which pervaded the room,' she reported.

Then she became aware that her son was spending restless nights. He told her that a 'little old man' would sit on his bed at night and tell him stories. Often she would hear footsteps approach her room at dead of night but when she opened her bedroom door, nobody would be there.

Things came to a head with a frantic knocking on the front door. A neighbour had just seen her son running through the garden to the cliff's edge. Panicking, Owena raced to the bottom of the garden. There she found her boy, struggling in a ditch – he had fallen into it trying to climb a wall overhanging a sheer drop into the ocean below.

Her husband now admitted that he knew the house was haunted. Local people had told him the story. The old man who had previously lived there had died in hospital claiming he had hidden his fortune in the overgrown garden. Before he died, he threatened to 'escape' and return to the cottage to claim it . . . and now his spirit would return by night, drawn to his treasure.

Owena was convinced it was this man who haunted her dream home and visited her son at night. She was sure her little boy's reckless race to the cliff's edge was somehow linked to the malign spirit's presence.

She was not prepared to put him at further risk. The Thomas family abandoned the cottage on the cliffs and left it to its ghost.

The girl in the blue gown

Most ghosts are described merely as apparitions, playbacks from the past as if on psychic videotape, but occasionally a ghost is reported to interact with the living, and will hold a conversation with them, such as the little boy in the last story may have experienced.

A similar experience also befell Mr John Williams, of Llanrug, near Caernarfon. Mr Williams reported that one Christmas Eve many years ago he was working as a clerk at a house auction in Anglesey and, left alone there, had a very strange experience.

After the sale was over and Mr Williams was waiting for his lift home, he helped himself to a glass of whisky from a secret stash he had been lucky enough to find in the butler's pantry, and then wandered out onto the terrace. There, to his surprise, he saw a young woman, standing in the shadow of a large ornamental eagle on the balustrade, softly illuminated by the moon.

Mr Williams describes her thus: 'She had on a blue evening gown and she had long yellow hair which seemed to shimmer, and it was arranged in a steep curtain as to conceal one half of her face completely.'

He greeted the young woman, found her friendly, and they enjoyed some easy conversation – 'it's hard to tell how long for' – but the girl never mentioned her name nor why she was there and when Mr Williams invited her in out of the cold she gave him the odd reply: 'I belong out here.'

Then Mr Williams offered her a dram of whisky.

'I would love some', she said. Mr Williams went to fetch another glass but when he returned, the girl had gone.

This was inexplicable and rather frustrating for a young man who has just met a pretty girl by moonlight, but he suspected nothing beyond the ordinary. However, when his driver, Dic, arrived to take him home and he told him about the girl, there was an uncomfortable silence.

At last, when they reached Mr Williams's home, he asked the driver: 'You've no idea who the girl was then?'

'You're not the first person to see her, you know,' said Dic. Then he explained: 'She's been dead for all of ten years. It was on a Boxing Day. There was a large party. After lunch they went shooting. She was reckoned a good shot, but she must have carried her gun awkwardly. She tripped and blew half her face off.'

'Half – her – face?' whispered Mr Williams.

'She was sozzled,' Dic continued. 'She used to carry a flask of whisky about with her. She was mad on the stuff. Hell of a craving for a girl of eighteen.'

It is an unhappy thought, that the spirit of a young girl should be bound to haunt a place where she had suffered such a tragic accident. The whisky could not have warmed her, but perhaps the short conversation with a young man who believed her to be a real and attractive girl might have offered her some comfort.

(Mr Williams subsequently learnt the name of the girl but I thought it better not to print it here, nor to mention the name of the house).

The wicked John Bodvol

Anglesey may be the most haunted place in Wales. Mrs Griffith, now of Hawarden in Flintshire, wrote about a spectral horse and rider which once haunted the island.

The spectre was seen at Marian Glas between Brynteg and Moelfre. Mrs Griffith is now eighty-four years of age and the story was told her by her grandmother, who had heard it from her own mother, who in turn had heard it from her grandmother, who had seen the ghost when she was a little girl – it is a tale of some antiquity.

Mrs Griffith wrote that the girl 'was standing in the doorway with her mother and a visitor who was about to leave, when her mother said to the visitor: "I wouldn't go just yet". Just then, "The Marian", as it was called, lit up and a white horse and rider appeared – and the rider had cloven hoofs.'

Mrs Griffith recalled that the spook was known by the name of John Bodvol and that her great-great-great-great-grandmother's sighting was certainly not the only one.

She told me: 'A midwife was walking along a country lane, having attended a mother-to-be, when she heard the clatter of hoofs coming beside her. It stopped beside her, and the rider asked if she wanted a lift. She noticed his cloven hoofs and refused.'

Very sensible of the midwife – one can guess where the devilish John Bodvol would have given her a lift to.

Mrs Griffith has one more story from Anglesey, this one involving an eerie, invisible ghost: 'I, myself, was told by a person (in my younger days) that when he was returning home on a dark night along a country lane in his horse and cart, his horse suddenly stopped dead and refused to move. The man tried all ways to urge him on but to no avail, so he stepped down and tried to lead the horse, which was very frightened and dripping with sweat.

'All of a sudden, a clanging of chains went across the lane in front of the horse – and only then did the horse proceed on his journey.'

The clanging of chains may have represented the chains of sin weighing down this lost spirit. Jacob Marley in Dickens's *A Christmas Carol* was all wrapped up in chains and a ghost at Llanfair Caereinion in Powys announced itself with a similar noise. In fact, ghosts accompanied by the sound of rattling chains have been reported in ancient times – by Roman writers. Perhaps the ghost haunting this lonely country lane on 'Mona' is even older than that of John Bodvol.

Author Dafydd Meirion later got in touch with the information that there was a notorious buccaneer of the name of John Wyn ap Hugh, of Bodfel, near Pwllheli, who was known as John Bodfal. He owned Ynys Enlli *(Bardsey Island)* which, according to Mr Meirion, became 'a pirate haven'. Mr Meirion is not saying for certain the phantom horseman with the cloven hoofs is 'John Bodfal', but he also knows of a legend which is strongly suggestive. The tale recounts that John Bodfal buried his treasure at Marian Glas. In ghostlore, hidden treasure seems to act as a kind of magnet for spirits; they can't leave the earth until the treasure is found, and that would explain why he haunted the spot. My thanks to Mr Meirion for his help. Subsequently I found a 1914 reference to the ghost of 'John Bodvel' haunting the area.

In two places at once

Derek Long, of Llansantffraid, wrote about a vivid experience he had while visiting Harlech castle:

'It was a few years ago on a glorious May afternoon; I was standing on the ramparts looking out over the bay. Not too many people were up there, so not a lot of noise to distract one. One moment a quiet sunny afternoon, the next moment I am in a snowstorm wearing chain mail and holding a spear! Still looking out over the bay, only now the sea was lapping at the base of the castle and a single-masted medieval ship was a few hundred yards out in the bay. I even felt the coldness of the weather!'

The vision lasted just a split second.

'When I realised what I was seeing – bang! – back to the sunny present.'

Derek, who describes himself as a spiritual healer and somebody 'used to unusual events', may simply have a strong imagination but he is convinced he experienced what he calls 'a time slip'. There are cases on record of people apparently finding themselves transported back to the past. Two ladies who claimed to have spent an hour or two wandering round eighteenth century Versailles in France is a famous example.

Was some sort of weird 'time slip' responsible for the odd experience of the McPheat family in Wrexham?

Gary McPheat told me that one evening at exactly 8.30 by the clock, his wife and children heard him come in through the door, put down his briefcase and announce in his customary fashion: 'Everyone all right?' Then they heard the door close again – and that was the last they saw of him for a while.

When he made an appearance half an hour or so later, his family asked him where on earth he had gone to? Why hadn't he come into the house? Gary looked at them blank-faced; what did they mean? When they told him that at 8.30pm they had heard him come in, he was nonplussed – he was in Llangollen at the time. He happened to glance at the clock, so there could be no mistake. He had apparently been in two places at once.

Although Gary McPheat's family hadn't actually seen him, apparitions of living people have frequently been recorded in Wales. In Welsh folklore such an apparition is called a lledrith.

A farmer, John Evans, had a similar experience to that of Gary McPheat in the nineteenth century. When he returned to his farm in Llanddewi Brefi after spending the day in Aberystwyth, he was told by his servants that he had been distinctly seen wandering around his fields – he, too, had been in two places at once.

'Well,' said Mr Evans, 'if you saw me, you only saw my spirit, for I have been away all day; now to see the spirit of a living man is not a bad sign.'

The idea that one's spirit can be separate from one's consciousness is an interesting one. What Mr Evans meant by it not being a bad sign was that if he had been dead, it would have meant his spirit was restless – maybe even in hell.

Mr McPheat's story sparked a memory for another reader, Susan Hanbury. She described an apparition of a living person, one she saw herself as a girl when she lived on a farm on Holy Island.

'The farmhouse had a few acres of land which became busy with campers during the summer holidays. It was usual to have people knocking on the door, asking for a place to camp or to borrow a spade, directions to the beach and so on. Mealtimes were seldom peaceful and I, being the youngest, would usually be expected to answer these calls.

'Well, one lunchtime, seated at the table, I noticed a lady passing the window, so I got up to answer the door. The front, dairy and back door of the farmhouse were all accessible to visitors and I opened each door but found no one there. I even thought the lady may have wandered into the garden. I could describe her in detail as I had seen her clearly: middle-aged, short, curly mid-brown hair, wearing a light green anorak with braid along the zip. No sign of her at all, so we finished our meal.

'Half an hour later I heard the front door knocker bang loudly and answered the door to see the lady I'd just described standing there. "Oh hello, you were here a while ago, weren't you?" I stated, not expecting the blank look from the visitor and family waiting in the car, as she replied that no, she hadn't been here before. They'd just arrived from Manchester and had chosen our campsite at random. My turn to look blank!'

The Ceffyl Dŵr

The quietest corners of Wales can hide the most unexpected things. Mr A.N. Foulkes, of Deganwy, wrote to tell me of a dramatic and terrifying apparition seen in a dip on a back road near Bryn-y-maen, south of Colwyn Bay.

Mr Foulkes is the man who saw the ghost of the dozing farmer in Glan Conwy. After hearing this story, a man Mr Foulkes describes as 'very stoic and unimaginative' was prompted to tell him of his own extraordinary experience. He said: 'My car was not taxed so I was going to work via back roads. Dawn had just broken, I drove down towards the dip, when all of a sudden this huge white horse flew straight over the hedge. I thought it must crash on my bonnet – it filled the windscreen!

'I stood on the brake, the car spun around, facing the way I had come, the engine cut out, but there was no bang. Somehow it missed me – in the split second I had to brake, it vanished. I know not where it could have gone. I shook with fear . . .'

Mr Foulkes later learnt, from a former work colleague, of another encounter with the fearsome phantom horse. This man's son and his girlfriend had been driving to Betws yn Rhos:

'They crossed the crossroads and descended into the dip when a huge white horse leapt over the hedge and seemed to be bound to collide with the front of their car. His girlfriend screamed and shut her eyes. He stamped on the brake and braced himself for the impact. Again the car spun around to face from whence they had come with the engine dead. The girl was shocked and crying and the lad was terrified.'

What possible explanation can there be for such a strange apparition?

There are other spectral horses in Welsh ghostlore; for example, a white horse with blood clots on its shoulders was supposed to haunt a lane near Llanymynech on the Shropshire border. There are also tales in Celtic folklore of mysterious horses called variously Pookah, Kelpie and, in Wales, Ceffyl Dŵr, which would gallop about the countryside.

Could the Bryn-y-maen horse be a Ceffyl Dŵr?

The Horror of Llofft Pinc

The following story has not seen print before. It is an even more alarming ghost story than that of the 'Ceffyl Dŵr above, and so makes a fitting conclusion to this parade of the Unexpected.

When Susan Hanbury wrote about the apparition she had seen as a young girl, she added a note in her letter that she had another story to tell, one concerning her former family home, should I be interested. Of course I was interested – but I wasn't prepared for the extremely eerie experiences Mrs Hanbury was able to relate. Although I was given permission to repeat names and locations, I felt it fairer to suppress them at this time, and hope to make a fuller study of the ghastly phenomenon described below.

Mrs Hanbury wrote: 'When my parents married they decided to do some decorating at the old farmhouse where my father was born and my mother still lives. During the night my father felt oppressed by something dark and threatening which seemed to be pressing on his neck and preventing him from breathing. He struggled and managed to get free, but kicked my mother in the process!

'In the morning light definite marks like bruises could be seen around my father's neck. Llofft Pinc, as the room is referred to, was thereafter kept as a visitor's room. Well, a short time later, my mother's parents visited and her father had the misfortune to experience the same disturbing sensation of being asphyxiated. There were marks, too, around my grandfather's throat.

'The room retained an unsettling atmosphere for some time. The house was being re-roofed and the plaster work removed from the walls of Llofft Pinc, which seemed to trigger a series of unexplained occurrences at the farm; at night the sound of hand bells could be heard downstairs and the hearth rug was rolled back several times. When the renovations were completed, the disturbances stopped.

'I personally remember one occasion, when I was a young girl. It was Christmas day and the family were returning from visiting my Uncle John Evans who was very poorly in Penrhos hospital, Holyhead. As we turned into the lane towards the farm we were puzzled to see every window illuminated at the house. We had not long had electricity and there were no lights in some of the rooms. My father switched off the engine and the van's lights as we looked at the house for a few minutes. Then we drove slowly towards the farm. As we arrived in the yard, the house was in darkness as we had left it. Uncle John died the next day.'